THE EMBROIDERED ARMOUR

ROBERTO PEREGALLI

THE EMBROIDERED ARMOUR

The Greeks and the Invisible

Drawings by Pierre le Tan

Pushkin Press
London

Pushkin Press
71-75 Shelton Street,
London WC2H 9JQ

Original text © 2008 RCS Libri S.p.A.

The Embroidered Armour first published in Italian as
La Corazza Ricamata in 2008.

This edition first published in 2013

ISBN 978 1 906548 33 9

All rights reserved. No part of this publication may be
reproduced, stored in a retrieval system or transmitted in
any form or by any means, electronic, mechanical,
photocopying, recording or otherwise,
without prior permission in writing from
Pushkin Press

Cover Illustration *The Song of the Sirens*
© Pierre le Tan
Frontispiece *Roberto Peregalli*

Set in 10.5 on 14 Monotype Baskerville
by Tetragon

Printed in Great Britain by CPI Group, UK

www.pushkinpress.com

CONTENTS

Introduction	13
The Ambiguities of The Visible	21
The Risk of Knowledge	37
The Deception of the Sphinx	57
The Invisible Connection	71
The Gift of Mnemosyne	81
The Charlatans of Heaven	95
The Paradox of Perception	107
The Double Vision	119
Heracles at the Crossroads	131
Postface	139
Notes	145
Bibliography	163
Illustrations	165

THE EMBROIDERED ARMOUR

The Greeks and the Invisible

To the night-ramblers, magicians, Bacchants, Maenads, Mystics …
Heraclitus *Fragments* B14

INTRODUCTION

THE LIFE OF HOMER[1] relates that the poet, standing by Achilles' tomb, wanted to see the hero in the armour made by Hephaestus, "brighter than blazing fire." (*Il.* XVIII 609) He was blinded by its brilliance. In return he was given wisdom.

The most skilful blacksmith had forged perfect armour, too beautiful to be seen by the eyes of men. The shield, the breastplate, the helmet, the greaves. A whole universe was sculpted within them. He decorated it with "earth, sky and sea, the tireless sun, the full moon, and all the constellations with which the skies are crowned." (*Il.* XVIII 483–485) And then the doings of men, places, wars.

Homer wanted to see. Hence he wished to know what was revealed. The disclosure, to the eyes, of that which is hidden concerns *truth*.[2]

Seeing for the Greeks is knowing. For that reason they are known as "the people of the eye".[3] That which is hidden is taken from the darkness of the invisible and brought into the light. The distance that separates that space and keeps it together generates the very possibility of knowledge. And, as such, it is precisely because of its 'tragic' essence, in that it presupposes that two incommensurable worlds, that of the visible and that of the invisible, enter into communication with one another.

Homer wishes to see Achilles' gleaming armour because the truth is inscribed within it. The splendour of that which is revealed to the light dims the vision. The dappled cloak of the shield constitutes the membrane which connects and divides the visible and the invisible. It is as dazzling as the thoughts of the gods.[4]

The concept of the *tragic* is produced and arranged within this space. The relationship of mortals to the world is based on what may be seen. But the truth of this is hidden, or only fitfully apparent. So for a people that connects knowledge with sight,[5] the relationship with truth becomes a tragic one. Privileging the visible as a place in which the fates of the world are played out, that which is invisible becomes deception,[6] fracture, mask. The invisible is an obstacle to knowledge. So it must be revealed. Truth is the revelation of that which is hidden.

Hence the way towards truth is the attempt to overcome that which is by its essence invisible. The Greeks want to see everything, to embrace the whole of the horizon with their eyes. In this 'seeing everything', the link between sight and knowledge becomes clear. That which is seen, insofar as it comes to light, is true. But the movement of appearing, condensed in the gaze, is possible only as emergence from hiding.

The words 'true' (*a-lethes*) and 'invisible' (*a-delon*) are at the same time mirror images and opposites. But their connection is evident: the negation of hiddenness certifies its existence. If that which is visible is true, it is true also that truth has its origin in that which cannot be seen. In the Greek world it is thus the ambiguous essence of *truth* which from the outset connects the visible and the invisible.

The 'invisible' is the shadow of the 'visible', its hidden bottom. The interesting thing about this word, *a-delon*, lies precisely in the difficulty of its appearance. The Greeks were sparing in their mentions of it until Plato. In Homer it occurs on one occasion

The weapons of Achilles

only, and few others in the authors that followed him, seldom with profound significance. This kind of Greek repression of the invisible is evident and inevitable. Sight is immediate knowledge and life. "The invisible," Aristotle will say, is "privation of potency".[7] Blindness, then, is an absence of completeness.

'Invisible' (*a-delon*) is a word rich in resonances.[8] It means uncertain, unknown, hidden, unclear, not manifest.[9] However, this negativity, parallel with that of 'truth' (*a-letheia*) with its privative 'a', seems to constitute its reverse, that of darkness. The invisible is part of all that cannot be mastered with the gaze, and thus, for a pre-Platonic Greek, with the mind. Being unmasterable, it constitutes a point of darkness. And it is upon this darkness, at the boundary between darkness and light, that Greek wisdom is structured.

The visible hides vast depths. But for the Greeks what matters is to remain on the surface.[10] From this derives the antinomy that forms the tragic element within their thought. Grasping the *invisible* means losing the lightness, the plasticity linked with sight, which represents for them an irrefutable presupposition.

Hence, capturing the invisible means leaving the structure of one world in order to enter another. The Greeks perceive this as a transgression, and, as such, a sin. Crossing the confines reserved for the possibilities of men means, for them, wanting to confront death, seeking in vain to overcome it.

At the same time Achilles' gleaming armour is what is most noteworthy, that which it is worth letting the gaze linger over. In a single moment, in its sudden gleam, the very possibility of knowledge unfolds. And furthermore, only insofar as it becomes visible does it produce wisdom.

This profound antinomy runs through Greek wisdom from its earliest beginnings.[11] Starting from the negative, from what for the Greeks was inexpressible, trying to discover its traces behind the curtain of the visible is perhaps one way of confronting it.[12] The path starts in Homer and concludes with Plato. It is a path towards darkness and death. The position with regard to the gaze is inverted. The importance of that which is not seen becomes the ontological constitution of an unattainable truth.

The subtle distinction between 'truth' (*a-letheia*) and 'invisible' (*a-delon*) vanishes. The invisible becomes that which is true. Homer's world which "knows no background"[13], the trust in the gaze, the truth of the visible, which can be a source of wisdom only in that it shows itself, are no longer enough. The gaze, resting on all that is visible, apparent, is fallacious. To capture the truth we must close our eyes to visible things. That is the gesture performed before Hades, the lord of the dead. The *tragic* origin of knowledge is apparent in all its force. Once the veil of the gaze has been removed, the flashing splendour of Olympus is inverted to become a vision of Hades.

The connection between truth and the invisible creates the arduous journey from that which is seen to that which is hidden. It is there that the mysteries, the word, Memory show themselves. With Plato this transformation is taken to its conclusion. In his dialogues, playing with words as an "accomplished Sophist",[14] he structures a new vision of the world.

The "race of men most capable of seducing us into life"[15] creates the soul, that hidden and nocturnal fragment that lies within man. The gleaming fascination of the images sculpted on Achilles' shield is translated 'in interiorem hominem'. The sight of the body is dimmed to make way for that of the soul. While *blindness*, supported by double vision, will no longer communicate with the gods.

The path that connects that which is seen to the invisible bottom of things, and its tortuous journey through the subtle space in which the Greeks placed knowledge and death, are the 'fabric' of this essay.

THE AMBIGUITIES OF THE VISIBLE

IN HOMER EVERYTHING IS VISIBLE. This abrupt assertion is intended to dismiss those interpretations which trace a few passages from the poems back to mysterious or irrational events. Mortals, immortals, souls and dreams, even Hades itself, are arranged within a horizon of light.[1] The distance that separates them is that which decrees a space defined by the gaze. And it is the gaze (in the sense of 'glance'), with its levels of depth, that defines the relationship of forces in the arrangement of the Homeric world. Sight is, in fact, the very possibility of knowledge. The same verbal paradigm of *idein* (to know) and *orao* (I see) demonstrates the extent to which the linguistic fabric is inscribed within this law.

But if, in Homer, everything can be seen, not all beings see in the same way and with the same intensity. The relationship between mortals and immortals is based on this tragic difference. The hierarchy determined by the intensity of sight establishes the distance of the inhabitants of Olympus from those who dwell "on the bounteous earth". The gods see more things than men. That is what makes them more powerful.

The Homeric arrangement of the world is therefore constituted by different ranges of intensity of vision. This gradation contains within itself the germ of the *invisible*. It is the reverse of the total knowability of the world. He who sees everything has the power to turn to his advantage that which is invisible to those with limited vision. The invisible is the measure of the distance of men from the gods.

"Who can see the comings and goings of a god, if the god does not wish to be seen? (*Od.* X 573–574) In a world in which everything is potentially visible, the possibility of eluding vision is a discriminating act. In it, mortals and immortals are playing at fate. But the former are not granted the ability to make themselves invisible. They are only able to hide.[2] But the game is not an even one. In the constant criss-cross of references with which men and the gods interact, the former can decipher only those actions which remain under the sign of the invisible.

In Book II of the *Iliad* (l. 305 ff), Odysseus reminds the Achaeans of the moment when, gathered under a plane-tree making sacrifices to the gods, "Zeus sent a fearful serpent out of the ground, with blood-red stains upon its back, and it darted from under the altar on to the plane-tree" and attacked a nest of birds. After swallowing them all, along with their mother, "when it had eaten both the sparrow and her young, the god who had sent it made him invisible; for the son of scheming Kronos turned him to stone." The episode is very important within the economy of the poem because it anticipates the victory of the Achaeans over Troy. And that is how the sign is interpreted by the soothsayer Calchas.

It is here, the only time in the two poems, that the word 'invisible' appears.[3] This is a disconcerting fact, but at the same time it contains the trace of an explanation. Zeus' gesture is an action: the red-backed snake becomes invisible. The action is directed at the mortals, who are obliged to interpret it as a sign, a great sign. Like all the actions in the *Iliad* and the *Odyssey*, it is enclosed within a visual horizon.[4] It is within this horizon that men and gods interact. The bond between the two connects the action with the open space beyond that which is seen.

The action, measuring the distance between mortals and immortals, grants the permanence of the invisible, and thus manifests the fate of mortals to remain dependent, obliged to interpret it as a sign. This sign, which pierces the visible in order to plunge itself into the darkness of the invisible, has a name: 'deception'. It is not a simple trick. It has a tragic dimension. For this reason it does not have a negative value in Homer. The gods deceive. Mortals, if they create deceptions, are wise. The fame of their feats (beginning with those of the cunning Odysseus) reaches all the way to the heavens.[5]

So deception concerns the very possibility of a space beyond the visible. It is the condition of that possibility. It is not solely the prerogative of the gods. It is universal. Its structure concerns sight as the very source of wisdom. Therefore it occurs as a tragic event. That which is not seen is that which is not known. In the subtle distinction of this equation, deception becomes a threat. In the relationship between sight, wisdom and deception, the full visibility of the Homeric world is dimmed.

Everything that comes from the heavens is deception, in that it is the work of fate and the gods: the magic threads, sleep, mist, souls, dreams. They are 'figures' bounded by the invisible. They suggest, but do not say.

The extreme proximity of mortals and immortals, their mutual interaction, mask a fundamental distance. The gods hold the secret of that which is not seen. That secret concerns knowledge and death.[6]

The Magic Threads

There is an invisible weaving that hangs over men and gods. It is cruel Moira, spinning with her thread the fate of mortals.[7] The gods have nothing with which to counter her. Magic threads are inscribed within this 'fabric': cloth, net, chains. Her power conditions the very existential dimension of man, making it a deception. The life of mortals is a deception of fate.

Moira's gesture has repercussions upon the entire hierarchy of the world. Women, mortal or immortal, weave. Men, on the other hand, make nets and chains. In the *Odyssey*, Penelope makes the cloth, Odysseus the net, Hephaestus the chains.

"Here is the *deception* she conceived in her heart. She set up a great frame in her room, and began to weave a measureless piece of fine cloth. During the day she would weave the large cloth, but at night she would unpick the stitches again." (*Od.* II 93 ff).

Penelope's gesture, which marks out the temporality of the *Odyssey*, includes an ambiguity. The time of the gesture is in fact the preparation of a deception. The cloth is enormous, literally 'measureless' (*perimetron*)[8], that is, it is unreal in character. Two goddesses, experts in deception, weave: Circe and Calypso.[9] Penelope's gesture refers us directly to this ambiguity. 'Weave', in fact, refers not only to cloth but also to deception.[10]

Penelope's cloth anticipates the future slaughter of the Suitors. The word 'weave' contains a dual resonance. The cloth brings death. It also has one other characteristic: it is fine.[11] The threads that hold it together are invisible. Therein lies its value. The invisible threads of the cloth are the threads of the fate of the Suitors.

Sister to the cloth is the net. "The net, an invisible mesh of bonds ... can seize anything yet can be seized by nothing."[12]

After Odysseus slaughtered the suitors, he "searched the whole court over carefully, to see if anyone had managed to hide and was still alive, but he found them all lying in the dust and weltering in their blood. They were like fishes which fishermen have taken from the sea in their thousand-eyed nets, and thrown on the beach to lie gasping for water till the heat of the sun makes an end of them." (*Od.* XXII 381–386)

The net is made of magic threads. Their invisible weave allows the fisherman to deceive the fish. The holes in the weave are actually thousands of eyes lying in wait for their prey. The art of fishing is based on mythological space. Within that space the fate of mortals is in question. Penelope's cloth is magically inverted into Odysseus' net.

This transformation is apparent in the *Agamemnon* of Aeschylus. The tapestry (the cloth) that Clytemnestra lays at the feet of her husband will be transformed into a net of Hades, "a boundless net like a fisherman's."[13] The spreading of the net's threads marks the passage from planned death to actual death.

On Olympus the magic threads are made in a different way. They are of iron, forged by Hephaestus the blacksmith. Their magic is more consistent. The fineness of these threads is miraculous, fashioned as they are from a material less pliable than linen. The finished product is called a 'chain'. But they are very particular chains (very different from the ones used by Zeus in his battle with the Titans).

The episode (*Od.* VIII 267 ff) is related by the bard Demodocos, and tells of the love between Ares and Aphrodite. Her husband Hephaestus, aware of the betrayal, *wove* an act of revenge. "He went to his smithy brooding mischief, put his great anvil on its block, and began to forge some chains which none could either unloose or break, in order to catch them. When he had finished his *snare*, outraged by Ares, he went into his bedroom and festooned the bed-posts all over with chains like cobwebs; he also let many hang down from the great beam of the ceiling. Not even a god could see them, so fine and subtle were they." When Ares and Aphrodite arrived, "they went to the couch to take their rest, whereon they were caught in the toils which cunning Hephaestus had spread for them, and could neither get up nor stir hand or foot, but found too late that they were in a trap."[14]

Ares had tried to deceive Hephaestus, but Hephaestus defeats him because his deception is invisible. His is a weave of chains as fine as cobwebs. So fine are they that no one, not even the gods, could see them. But the material is so resilient that, once someone has fallen into their trap, they can't get out again. Just as the spider grabs the insect indirectly by means of extremely laborious and invisible work, Hephaestus traps his adulterous wife and her immortal lover.

His weave of threads has one other characteristic: it is circular. The circle is disorienting in that it has neither beginning nor end. Encirclement is a deception because, the centre remaining empty, it becomes invisible.[15]

The episode of Hephaestus concludes with the divine and inextinguishable laughter of all the Olympians summoned to witness the scene. And this seems to cancel out its tragic repercussions. Not so. Here the mortals are absent. But, by contrast, human destiny increases its tragic properties. If punishment for the immortals is a farce which provokes laughter, the magic threads, when used for mortals, become an instrument of death.

The deception of Hephaestus

Sleep

Sleep is a god, the brother of Death. He reigns over Night.[16] His power extends over men and gods. His weapon is invisible. With it he reaches all the way to Zeus. Being capable of putting Zeus to sleep, he strips him of his ability to see, and hence his omniscience. This is the only deception capable of taking hold of Zeus. He who sees everything closes his eyes. His greatness becomes nothing.

But Sleep's deception does not act in the same way on mortals and immortals. For the latter, Sleep is an invisible bond that puts them hors de combat. Their vigilance vanishes. Like a net, Sleep spreads and envelops everyone in its meshes. Because his sister Death has no power over them, Sleep becomes the most dangerous of the gods. The epithet "sweet" which Homer confers upon him (*Il.*, XIV, 242) underlines his ambiguity. Sleep is an enticing deception.

The relationship between Sleep and the mortals is very different. Penelope says: "But no one can do without sleep for ever. The gods have given it its allotted space in our daily lives, like everything else on this bounteous earth."[17]

In this case the invisible bonds of Sleep have a beneficial outcome. They distract men from their troubles. They allow people to forget for a moment that which cannot be forgotten, because it is part of their essence as mortals: cruel Moira. For them, too, Sleep is a deception.[18]

While in the case of the gods it is Sleep as god that pours its enchanted weapon over their eyelids, in the case of men any god can do the same. Sleep is thus a seeming death. It is a curious fact that only those who can die sleep untroubled.

Mist

"Hera (...) you need not fear that any god or man will see us: I shall hide you in a golden mist so dense that even the sun, whose rays give him the keenest sight in the world, will not see us through it."[19]

This is the voice of Zeus. He *weaves* a deception. Its name is 'mist'. It renders gods, men and things invisible. Not even the Sun, the god who is the sky's eye, can enter it. It is a divine instrument, an act to deceive. It appears frequently in the Homeric poems, to different ends.

It conceals the appearance of the gods. Thus Thetis appears to Achilles: "She rose as it were a mist out of the waves."[20] Thus Apollo comes towards Patroclus "enshrouded in thick mist."[21]

It is sent by the gods to hide a mortal. Paris is rescued from his duel with Menelaus by Aphrodite who "hid him under a cloud of mist."[22] Idaeus is saved by Hephaestus wrapping him in a cloud of mist.[23] Athena hides Odysseus from the Phaeacians by pouring "a thick cloud of mist"[24] around him. When he reaches Ithaca, Athena throws mist around him, to make him unrecognisable.[25]

It is sent by the gods to obscure the sight of mortals. Thus Poseidon pours mist over Achilles' eyes when he is fighting, to save Aeneas.[26]

It is taken away from mortals by the gods, so that they may see better. Thus Athena lifts the mist from the eyes of Diomedes, that he may know both gods and mortals.[27]

Mist thus creates a distance between mortals and immortals. An instrument of separation, even when it brings men closer to a higher condition, it stresses their underlying impotence. Mist, in fact, is the sight of men. It is because of it that they are unable to see everything. Their knowledge is limited. The intervals of light that the gods allow them constitute the chance nature of a knowledge that tragically roots itself within its 'misty vision'.

Souls and Dreams

There is a word in Homer that lies between the visible and the invisible: *eidolon* (apparition, phantom). Its root is *orao* (I see) and its meaning is obscure. Two things are defined by this word: the soul and dreams.

Eidolon, like *eidos* (figure, appearance), is the 'image', but with a hint of unreality.[28] It is the apparition of a thing, its simulacrum. The image, in fact, is what we see of a thing that doesn't exist. It is an absence of being. As such it represents a deception.

After Patroclus is dead, Achilles, grieving, lies down "on the shore of the sounding sea." He falls asleep, and is visited by the "sad spirit (*psyche*) of Patroclus, as he had been in stature, voice, and the light of his beaming eyes, dressed, too, as he had been dressed in life." Achilles speaks to it:"'Why, true heart, have you come here? Draw closer to me, let us once more throw our arms around one another, and find sad comfort in the sharing of our sorrows.' He opened his arms towards him as he spoke and would have clasped him in them, but there was nothing, and the spirit (*psyche*) vanished as a vapour, gibbering and whining into the earth. Achilles sprang to his feet, smote his two hands together, and lamented saying, 'Of a truth even in the house of Hades there are ghosts and phantoms (*psyche kai eidolon*) that have no life in them.'"[29]

What is the essence of this shade? It "has no connection with the thinking and feeling soul."[30] In Homer, *psyche* is only the soul while it animates man, while it keeps him alive. Separated from the body, it appears as *eidolon*, phantom, image.

It is this soul-image that Hermes, the messenger-thief, guides to the realm of the dead with his golden rod. A cortege of shades accompanies the mysterious journey from the surface to the depths of the earth.[31] But the soul as image is a deception. Resembling the person from whom it comes, as visible as that person, it has no consistency. Achilles tries to embrace Patroclus' soul, Odysseus that of his mother. Both clutch the void. It no longer has its mind: its memories and sensations are erased. It has no power over the living, it awaits nothing. Parted from time, it wanders in a dark cave as a blind image.

Its contacts with the surface world are broken. It appears to the living only in dreams. The realm of dreams constitutes the bond between mortals and the shades of mortals. "Pindar tells us that the body obeys Death, the almighty. But the image of the living creature lives on ... for it is sleeping when the limbs are active, but when the body is asleep it often reveals the future in a dream."[32]

Dreams, like the soul, are *eidola*, images. They are sent by the gods. As Penelope falls asleep, and lies on her bed "within the gates of dream," grey-eyed Athena makes "a vision (*eidolon*) in the likeness of a woman. (...) It came into her room by the hole through which the thong went for pulling the door to, and hovered over her head, and spoke to her."[33]

Dreams are seen, they speak with the sleeper, they have a human face. Masks of Hermes, like him they too are messengers. They herald, they deceive. "Stranger, dreams (*oneiroi*) are very curious and unaccountable things, and they do not by any means invariably come true. There are two gates through which these unsubstantial fancies proceed; the one is of horn, and the other ivory. Those that pass through the gate of ivory are fatuous, but those from the gate of horn inform the dreamer of what will come to pass."[34]

They are not, as Artemidorus will later say, "a movement or condition of the mind that takes many shapes and signifies good or bad things that will occur in the future."[35]

They do not come from any assumed human interiority, they descend from heaven.

Evanescent physical presences are, like all things that can be seen, a source of knowledge. But arranged in an interregnum between the visible and the invisible, they are not always images of truth. Bound up "with swoons, with dreams, with ecstasy,"[36] they can sometimes be a source of deception. Mortals must refer to them, although knowing that, since they come from the gods, they cannot put their full trust in them. Their fate is to listen to the voices of ghosts, in order to decipher a trace of their own mortal condition.

Souls and dreams dwell in Hades.[37] It is the mythological space of Erebus, the nocturnal and subterranean dimension of the world. "And there, all in their order, are the sources and the ends of gloomy earth and misty Tartarus and the unfruitful sea and starry heaven, loathsome and dank, shunned even by the gods. It is a great gulf, and if once a man were within the gates, he would not reach the floor until a whole year had passed, but cruel blast upon blast would carry him this way and that. And this marvel is awful even to the deathless gods. There stands the awful home of murky Night wrapped in dark clouds." (Hesiod, *Theogony*, 736ff.).

Within this scenario, souls and dreams constitute a people of images, bound to night and death. Gods have relations with mortals in dreams. Their presence enigmatically heralds the future. Souls, though, which seldom appear to the living in dreams, are the only remaining trace of mortals after death. Their presence constitutes the essence of the life of man as a fleeting shadow, imprisoned in darkness.

THE RISK
OF KNOWLEDGE

I N A SPACE within which men have a 'misty vision', the ability to see farther represents the extreme possibility of defeating the darkness of death. Homer's world is set out upon the surface of the gaze, but there is another way, nocturnal and profound, linked to vision—the Mysteries—in a mirror image which constitutes the vertical dimension of the god-man relationship. The coffer of Olympus opens to reveal hidden treasures.

Pindar says (Fr 137): "Happy is he who sees these things and goes beneath the earth; he knows the end of life and he also knows its Zeus-given beginning."[1] For mortals, this is the opportunity to overcome their destiny. They perish, in fact, "because they cannot connect the beginning with the end."[2]

The promise of the Mysteries is to show the possibility of closing the circle, broken for men into a straight line. They are a visual manifestation. The light that they give off is the dazzling splendour of that possibility. The secrecy in which they are enwrapped, still alive in Plutarch, indicates the difficulty of its negotiability: "the awesome rites ... which no one may transgress in any way or inquire into or speak about." ('*Hymn to Demeter*' 478)[3] Their reality is alien to the word.

They are a nocturnal feast that refers to a number of divinities. In the Attic calendar they occurred twice a year, in spring and autumn, with the waning moon. The name that defines them is *Mysteria*. Like *mystes* ('initiate') and *mystikos*, this word derives from the verb *myeo*, I initiate (into the Mysteries). But this verbal formation comes from *myo*, the meaning of which, 'I close my eyes', is an important clue.

"The monuments ... show us that we must not think here of a silence (closing the mouth) in the presence of the *arreton*, but a ceremony of closing the eyes. Herakles is seated with his head totally covered. The *Mysteria* begin for the *mystes* when, as sufferer of the event (*myoymenos*), he closes his eyes, falls back as it were into his own darkness, enters into the darkness. The Romans use the term 'going-into,' '*in-itia*'(in the plural), not only for this initiating action, the act of closing the eyes, the *myesis*, which is exactly rendered as *initiation*, but for the *Mysteria* themselves. A festival of entering into the darkness, regardless of what issue and ascent this initiation may lead to: that is what the *Mysteria* were in the original sense of the word." [4]

The Mysteries are the figuration of a journey. Closing his eyes, the initiate opens himself up to the realm of darkness. But Pindar's lines are clear in this regard: what awaits the initiate is a vision. And in the '*Hymn to Demeter*', the oldest testimony to the Mysteries, the observation is analogous: "Blessed is he of all the people on earth who has seen these things." [5] How are we to explain the contrast?

Colli speaks of a "festival of knowledge". And he interprets the two passages in a metaphysical sense, quibbling with "the moderns". They, "convinced that only that which all may see can be seen, object that this expression is used to refer to all sacred objects, to images of the gods, to the symbolic representations that appeared in the Eleusinian ritual."[6]

But in this way the second part of Pindar's fragment becomes incomprehensible. "It really does seem hard to imagine—although the poets doubtless exaggerate—that the contemplation of the effigy of a goddess grants a large

Heracles veiled

number of initiates knowledge of the beginning and end of life."[7] Vision, for Colli, is a symbolic form of the act of supreme knowledge, in the style of the great speculative mystics.[8]

Hesiod calls the Mysteries "terrible to behold."[9] The proof reserved for initiates puts vision at risk. The contrast then becomes yet more obscure, but also concrete rather than mystical.

Being initiated into the Mysteries, closing the eyes. The Mysteries are inexpressible. The vision that is manifested is kept secret in that it cannot be translated into words. It is terrible. In order to receive it one must close one's eyes.

It seems to be an insoluble riddle. But knowledge is a riddle. To see is to know, insofar as to see is to close one's eyes. In this gesture the relationship between man and god is played out once again. Closing the eyes in order to see is the deception of knowledge in its ritual manifestation. In the 'visible' night of the festival an 'invisible' light is unveiled.[10]

Three objects hint symbolically at the event of the Mysteries: the veil, the mirror, the mask.

The Veil

"The veil recalls concealment of secret things; the unveiling is a revelation, a knowledge, an initiation." [11] The head of the initiate is completely covered.[12] Closing the eyes and putting on the veil thus have an analogous significance.

The veil closes off the gaze from the world. It is an introduction into darkness. An invisible wall, it distances things in order to bring them closer. In two ceremonies the veil appears as a symbolic figure: weddings and funerals. "In antiquity, when the bride was given over to her betrothed, she was covered like the departed, destined to the underworld at the moment of being given over to death, and so it is with the *mystes*."[13]

In the cycle of creation and destruction, the veil is a symbol of knowledge in the relationship between mortals and immortals, heaven and earth. But this does not entirely cancel out the possibility of vision. "Il tamise en effet la lumière pour la rendre perceptible."[14]

The initiate is thus ready to see that which is manifested before him: an inexpressible mimicry that shows divine matters. Attaining sacred unions, he "knows the end of life and he knows the Zeus-given beginning."

This happens at night, in the dark. "The nocturnal element was not limited to the covering of the *mystes* in the first moment of initiation. The *Mysteria* were so essentially nocturnal that in them every aspect of the night was experienced, even that power residing solely in the night, the power to engender the light as it were, to help it come forth. They were not merely a nocturnal festival, they actually—or at least it seems so—solemnised the feeling of being shut in by the night, culminating in a sudden great radiance."[15]

One myth on the subject of the "sacred marriage" related by Pherecydes (B2) clarifies the complex symbology of the veil. This is the marriage of *Zas* and *Chthonie* in the presence of *Chronos*. *Zas*, an etymological form of *Zeus*, is the ruler of Heaven. *Chthonie*, from *chthon* (earth), is the Underworld; *Chronos* is Time.

"For [*Zas*] they make the houses, many and great. And when they had finished providing all this, and also furnishings and men-servants and maid-servants and all else required, when all is ready, they carry out the wedding. On the third day of the wedding, Zas makes a veil, large and fair, and on it he embroiders astutely Earth (*poikillei*) and Ocean and his dwelling... 'Wishing this to be your marriage, I honour you with this. Therefore receive my greeting and be my wife.' This they say was the first unveiling ceremony (*anakalypteria*), and hence arose the custom among gods and men. And she repaid him, receiving the veil (*to pharos*) from him..."[16]

I should like to begin with the word *anakalypteria*. *Kalyptein* means 'to veil, to conceal'. *Anakalyptéein* means 'to unveil'. *To anakalypterion* is the gift that the bride received the day she appeared for the first time without a veil.[17] The *anakalypteria* are a Greek nuptial feast. In the rite, the bride removes her veil and the groom offers a gift. As a feast it occupies the opposite pole of the Mysteries, insofar as the unveiling of the latter corresponds to the veiling of the former.[18]

In Pherecydes' myth, however, there is one very important detail. The gift that *Zas* offers his bride is another veil (*pharos*). More opaque, *pharos* also means 'cloak'. It is embroidered with images of Earth and Ocean.

What we are witnessing is thus both an unveiling and a veiling. This is followed, in the myth, by a change in the name of the bride: from *Chthonie* she becomes *Gê* (Earth). *Chthonie*, subterranean divinity, invisible depth, is transformed into *Gê*, surface, appearance.

The link with the Mysteries becomes apparent. The subsequent veiling of *Chthonie* recalls that of the initiate. But this myth refers to something deeper. The culminating moment of the rite is the unveiling of *Chthonie*. The invisible depth opens up to Heaven. 'Unveiling' in Greek is also called *aletheia*, truth. In the unveiling of *Chthonie* it is truth that is at stake.

But depth cannot be captured in its essence. This is the meaning of the gift of *Zas*. The veil that the celestial divinity offers to *Chthonie* is the manifestation of the impossibility of guessing depth without the veil of appearance.

The *invisible* should not be unveiled. For whom? Only mortals know the distance that unites Heaven and Earth. Linked with this is the nakedness of *Chthonie*. The veil of *Zas* has interwoven Ocean and Earth. These are what we see, an appeal from the gods. But we know that what we see is appearance. The invisible depth of *Chthonie* is the truth of things, which we can read through the veil of *Zas*.[19] But over time *Chthonie* comes to be called *Gê*, earth, surface.

The veil of *Zas* is a deception. Only through deception is the invisible made manifest to men.

The episode of Odysseus and Leucotea falls within this complex symbology: "Take off those clothes, leave your raft for the winds to play with, and swim for your life to the Phaeacian coast, where deliverance awaits you. Here: take this veil and wind it round your waist. With its divine protection you need not be afraid of injury or death. But directly you touch the dry land with your hands, undo the veil and throw it into the wine-dark sea."[20] The unveiling and the subsequent veiling of Odysseus are very close to the sacred ceremonies. It appears, in fact "that this veil was the purple ribbon that was given to the initiates".[21]

The Mirror

There is an Orphic fragment that speaks of Dionysus and a mirror: "While [Dionysus] contemplated his changeling countenance (*nothon eidos*) in an estranging mirror (*antitypo katoptro*) they destroyed him with an infernal knife."[22]

This fragment describes an action in a succinct form. The dominant element is the "estranging mirror". This is given to Dionysus by the Titans along with other "toys".[23] The gift of the Titans is revealed to be a deception. Dionysus, looking into the mirror, is distracted, and the Titans are thus able to strike him by treachery. But why is Dionysus enchanted by the mirror?

Dionysus sees a deceitful image reflected in the mirror. Of this image, Proclus says (in Plat. *Tim.* 33b): "But long ago the theologians also accepted the mirror (*to esoptron*) as a symbol of the receptivity to intellectual fulfilment of the universe. For this reason they say that Hephaestus made a mirror for Dionysus. When he looked into it and saw his own image, he proceeded to the universal divisible creation." And he adds (in Plat. *Tim.* 29a-b): "Just as, therefore, Orpheus fashions replicas (*eidola*) of Dionysus which preside over the process of becoming and have received the entire form (*to eidos olon*) of the paradigm."[24]

There is specularity between the image of the god and the plurality of things. Seeing his image, Dionysus sees the world.[25] *Katoptron* and *esoptron* (mirror) contain the root *op-* of *opsis* (sight). *Katopter* means 'explorer', 'observer'. The Latin translation, *speculum*, is still more illuminating.

"The Latin word for mirror (*speculum*) has given us the verb 'to speculate'; and originally speculation was scanning the sky and the related movement of the stars by means of a mirror. The Latin for star (*sidus*) has also given us the word 'consideration' which, etymologically, means to scan the stars as a whole. Both abstract nouns which now describe highly intellectual activities are rooted in the study of the stars reflected in mirrors. It follows, then, that mirrors, as reflecting surfaces, should be the basis of a wealth of symbolism relating to knowledge."[26]

Both the Greek and Latin words contain a powerful cosmological resonance. Through the gaze, reflected, in the face of heaven, vision becomes knowledge. The mirror, like the veil, becomes the membrane through which the hidden essence of things becomes visible.[27]

Colli says: "The mirror is a symbol of illusion, because what we see in the mirror does not exist in reality, it is merely a reflection. But the mirror is also a symbol of knowledge, because by looking at myself in the mirror I know myself. And it is also such a symbol in a more refined sense, because all knowledge is putting the world in a mirror, reducing it to a reflection that I possess."[28]

Four elements emerge from the Orphic fragment: the god's enchantment with the image reflected in the mirror; the contents of the image: the face of the god and the plurality of the world; the gift of the mirror as a *deception*; the ambiguous relationship between vision and knowledge.

We find two of these elements interwoven in another myth related by Ovid, that of Narcissus. (*Metamorphoses* III 345 ff) "Liriope, having fallen pregnant, had given birth to a child, who at his birth was already adorable, and had called him Narcissus. In due course she consulted the seer: 'Tell me,' she asked, 'will my baby live to a ripe old age?' 'Yes,' he replied, 'so long as he does not know himself.'"

Once he has grown, he despises all women. Coming upon a pool of water, as he drinks, "he is suddenly filled by the form that he sees reflected in it, he hopes for a love that has no form, he mistakes the shadow for the substance. Stunned, he stares at himself and unable to take his eyes away he remains motionless as a statue of Parian marble. Lying on the ground, he contemplates the twin stars, his own eyes, and the hair worthy of Bacchus, worthy even of Apollo, and the youthful cheeks and the ivory neck and the gem of a mouth and the blushing white mingled with creamy whiteness. And admires all that makes him an extraordinary being. Unwittingly, he desires himself; he adores, but he adores himself, and as he yearns it is for himself that he yearns, he both lights and burns. How many times does he try in vain to kiss the treacherous spring! How many times does he plunge his arms into the water to throw his arms around the neck that he sees but cannot grasp! He doesn't know what it is that he sees, but the sight still fires him with passion, and the very error that deceives his eyes excites his lust. Innocent fool, why do you try to grasp a fleeting image? The one you yearn for doesn't exist, the one you love will flee if you turn away. What you see is the shadow, the reflection of your face, a reflection with nothing of its own; with you it came, with you it stays; with you it would leave – if you could ever go!"

At last he exclaims exhaustedly, "This is me!" Now he knows, his image no longer deceives him, but the desire is ever greater to know himself. And he dies.

Water, like the mirror, reflects an image. This image is a *deception*. Made of nothing, impalpable as Homer's souls and dreams, it enchants. It is sent by the gods to punish Narcissus for his indifference. What is at stake is the relationship between mortals and immortals. The punishment consists in a deception, a strange deception concerning knowledge. Narcissus' vision is the reflection of something that cannot be revealed to men, the essence of which remains invisible. The veil of water, as the sole means of knowledge but at the same time a deception, constitutes a risk, from which one can die.

In the Orphic fragment, on the other hand, it is a god that looks in the mirror. For that reason the relationship with mortals is mediated to a greater degree. Dionysus looks at his image

The myth of Narcissus

and sees the world reflected. As with the veil of Zas, this too is appearance. The 'deceitful image' enchants the god, because it shows him as the author of an illusion, our world. This is the reflection of a reflection insofar as it is revealed in the very image of Dionysus reflected by the mirror.

But this image of the world has significance for men. What they see is merely appearance. And that is what knowledge consists in. Dionysus looks with enchantment at the images that appear in the god's toy. He does not know that in it he is contemplating himself. Herein lies the first deception. It is the reason why the Titans are able to surprise him. But the god cannot die. The creation that he looks at is that which we believe to be real, while in fact it is merely a reflection. This is the other face of the deception. Ploughing the abyss of appearance and reaching the invisible light is the supreme task of mortals, where the relationship with the gods is concerned.

The Mask

The veil and the mirror. A third object of the Mysteries, linked to Dionysus, is the mask (*prosopon*). *Prosopon* also means face, semblance, countenance. The root is the *op-* of *opsis*, sight. The Latin translation is *persona*, its specific meaning is mask, but in a broader sense also character, persona, personality.

The most disconcerting fact is that both for the Greeks and the Romans, terms such as 'face', 'character' or 'person' are generic derivatives of 'mask', an object that precisely conceals the face, substituting for it.

The mask is above all bound up with the god. "It was, I take it, as Master of Illusions, that Dionysus came to be patron of a new art, the art of the theatre. To don a mask is the easiest way of ceasing to be oneself. The theatrical use of the mask presumably grew out of its magical use: Dionysus became in the sixth century the god of the theatre because he had long been the king of the masquerade."[29]

Bringing it back, as an object, to a magical and religious function, Dodds stresses the relationship that is established between man and god. The mask is a visible membrane that conceals and at the same time suggests (*semainei*). It conceals the face of its wearer. Turning him into someone else, it causes him to leave himself. In this sense it is a vehicle of wisdom.

The mask has fixed features. Frozen in its immobility, its eye-sockets are empty. In the relationship established between man and god it creates an ambiguity: while approaching, as a symbol of identification, at the same time it distances. It is only when he puts on the mask that a mortal, by denying himself, can make himself a god.

The gods have become invisible. They no longer banquet with mortals. In the Mysteries, the mask is the sign of their presence. It suggests the *invisible*. Thus revealing its illusory character, its mirror essence, it deceives. By bringing man out of himself, it breaks the barriers that locate him between animal and god. He can identify with one or the other. For that reason too, animal masks appear frequently in the Greek world.

The mask is appearance. Like the veil and the mirror, it provides a sense that the truth lies in the depth, and is concealed. Being without a mask (*aprosopon*) thus has a negative connotation. The late Greek text that speaks of the slave as *aprosopon* probably refers to this state of being without a mask and, by virtue of being without a mask, without a persona. It is the most serious insult that a Greek can make to a man[30] because "everything deep loves a mask".[31]

The realm of the mask is nocturnal and illusory: the night, the Mysteries, the theatre. In the funeral rites it imitates what it hides, the face of the dead, by entering a relationship with the living. In the Mysteries and in the theatre it transforms man into animal or god.

Over ten scenes, a famous fresco in the Villa of the Mysteries in Pompeii shows a young woman's initiation into the Mysteries. One of these shows "an old Silenus who, sitting on a double plinth, holds, looking away with a forced movement of his whole body, a white object, silver, in the form of a bowl, into which a young man bending over behind the back of the Silenus, gazes intensely, holding the object with one hand under the bottom; close to the Silenus, on the ground, lies a tympanum, and behind the young man a companion holds aloft, motionless, a Dionysiac mask."[32]

The atmosphere is filled with suspense. The forced gesture of the old Silenus, the gaze that awaits the revelation of the fate of the young man who holds the mask aloft, the astonishment of the one looking into the bowl construct the metaphysics of the event. The sense of estrangement is increased by the fact that none of the characters present is looking upon the action that is being played out. The Silenus holds the bowl and looks elsewhere, at a fixed point in the distance; the youth holding the mask stares steadily in front of him; the gaze of third, looking into the bowl, is bounced towards a precise but seemingly enigmatic vanishing point.

It is in this gesture that the event is measured. The bowl acts as a concave mirror. It reflects not, as we might expect if the mirror were flat, the image of the youth looking into it, but (and this has been calculated mathematically) the mask behind him.

The surprised gaze is thus justified by the unexpected vision. But that is not all. The mask is a Dionysiac mask, and thus belongs to the god. In the process of reflection the youth is identified with the image of the god reflected in the bowl. The mask therefore constitutes the visible link with the invisible presence of the god.

The youth is permitted to approach the god, but the bridge from appearance to the invisible is made of reflections, masks, mirrors. The astonishment that takes hold of him as he looks is the risky gift of knowledge.

The tragic enchantment of these elements recurs in the myth of the Gorgon. There, the motif of "the eye, the gaze, the reciprocity of seeing and being seen."[33] The face of the Gorgon is a mask. Anyone who gazes upon it is turned into stone. "To see the Gorgon is to look her in the eyes and, in the exchange of gazes, to cease to be oneself, a living being, and to become, like her, a Power of death."[34] This killing gaze has empty sockets.

Unlike the mask that is worn to imitate the god, "this figure reproduces the effect of a mask by merely looking you in the eye. It is as if the mask had parted from your face, had become separated from you, only to be fixed facing you, like your shadow or reflection, without the possibility of your detaching yourself from it."[35] A self-doubling, like the image of Narcissus in the reflecting water, but also radical otherness, the Gorgon's death-head constitutes the horrific aspect of the mask, its link with knowledge and death.

'Closing the eyes' (*myein*): in the rite of the Mysteries a path is walked from darkness to light. The thresholds of the visible open up to the *invisible*. At the same time, what is shown to the initiate is a vision. Hence the apparent contradiction with *myein*: how can one 'see' if the object of the rite is to 'close the eyes'?

The three objects I have mentioned—the veil, the mirror, the mask—cast light on the mystery and symbolise the path of the initiate. The *invisible* is manifested only through reflected signs. What we see is appearance (Heaven and Earth embroidered on Zas's cloak, the plurality of things in Dionysius' mirror, the mask of Silenus in the silver bowl). But if we 'close our eyes' to this, we can grasp the suggestion of something else.

What is at issue here is the relationship between men and gods. For the former it is the risk of knowledge. Being able to endure the play of reflections, confronting their illusory nature. And besides, no other way is granted to them.

For the latter, this is the deception made to men by 'cruel Moira'. Invisible, they hint from their deep seat through deceitful objects, terrible 'toys'. The most disconcerting of these reproduces the invisible face of the god. Wearing it is a weighty matter. But slaves alone go without masks.

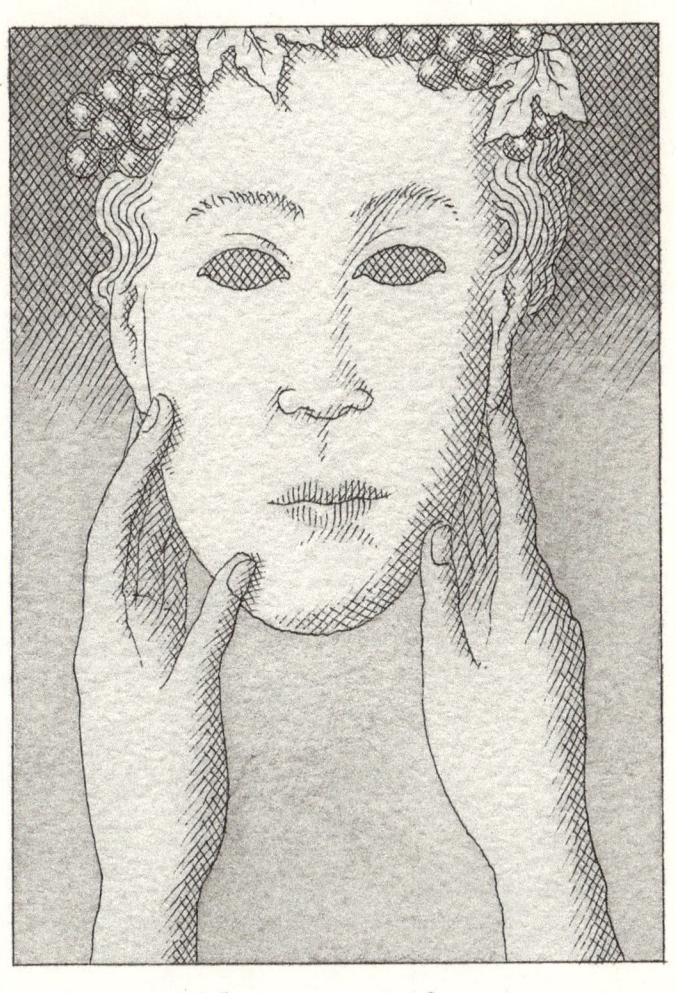

The Silenus and the mask

THE DECEPTION
OF THE SPHINX

T HE LIGHT OF HOMER, the nocturnal brilliance of the Mysteries, problematically connect what is seen to an invisible background. This is the relationship between Heaven and Earth, men and gods. The light released is the possibility of a knowledge that finds in dazzling revelation the deception of its dual essence: visible surface, hidden depth.

In the dramatic origins of tragedy, the tension is concentrated. Man, reflected in himself, is expressed as the riddle in the figure of the blind seer.

Creon says at the beginning of *Oedipus the King* (l 130–131): "The Sphinx who sings deceptive things (*poikilodos*) forced us to see what was near (*to pros posi*), obscuring the invisible (*taphane*)." Oedipus replies (l 132): "From the start I will bring this to light." These lines speak of the 'invisible' (*to aphanes*). Interwoven with this are the Sphinx, deception, man.

The Sphinx is *poikilodos*. *Poikilos* is "the sheen of a material or the glittering of a weapon, the dappled hide of a fawn, or the shining back of a snake mottled with darker patches. This many-coloured sheen or complex of appearances produces an effect of iridescence, shimmering, an interplay of reflections which the Greeks perceived as the ceaseless vibrations of light."[1] Hence the meaning of 'deceptive', which polarises the journey of the word between light and deception.[2]

The Sphinx sings a riddle (Pindar Fr 177d). Anyone who fails to solve it dies. Its content is this: which creature is "two-legged, three-legged and four-legged" (*dipous, tripous, tetrapous*)?" 'Oedipus' (*Oidipous*), the man with the ambiguous name—"with the bandaged foot" (*oidos pous*) but also "he who knows" (*oida*)—has solved the riddle: the answer is "man".[3]

This is all part of 'that which is near'(*to pros posi*). It is appearance, surface. As such it is set out within a temporal dimension which precedes the very beginning of the tragedy. In the prologue Oedipus has already solved the riddle, he has become king. The Sphinx has been defeated. But its power is not yet over. Men have forgotten what is 'invisible' (*to aphanes*).

The riddle of the Sphinx is thus a *deception*. Its revelation leads to a weightier riddle, whose antecedent was only its apparent face. The Sphinx had formulated a question about man, a fatal question. Oedipus' answer grasps only its surface appearance. Man remains a riddle.

The gods have fled, the Age of Gold is long gone. Caught between two extremes, bound to the earth but with his gaze turned to heaven, man is a riddle. Oedipus' tragedy is that riddle's solution: 'the invisible' (*to aphanes*).

The transition from 'that which is near' to the 'invisible', moving from one pole to the other: this is the 'tragic' sense of Oedipus' fate. In this passage his gesture becomes essential: blinding.

When Creon tells Oedipus that the Thebans have neglected 'the invisible', he replies: "From the start I will bring this to light." (1 132) Oedipus' task from the outset has been to bring the invisible to light. That task belongs to the wise man. And as such, having solved the riddle of the Sphinx, he is recognised by Thebes.

His path is interwoven with that of another enigmatic figure, Teiresias.[4] He first appears in the *Odyssey* (X 493 ff), as a "blind prophet" (*mantis alaos*) whose "mind is unimpaired, for

Persephone has granted him, and him alone, wisdom (*nóon*) in death". Even in this passage the figure of Teiresias seems to be endowed with exceptional powers. The only deviation from the Homeric conception of *psyche*, the sage of Thebes preserves his (*nous*) even after death.

Teiresias is a blind soothsayer. As a soothsayer he sees the invisible. In order to have this power he has become 'blind'. The knot that binds the vision of the invisible and blindness shows the pessimistic foundation of Greek wisdom.[5] Why does it involve this serious forfeit, so serious for the Greeks that they gave seeing and knowledge a common origin? In this seeming antinomy there is something primal and terrible.

There are two myths concerning Teiresias' blindness. The first relates that, for observing two snakes in the act of copulation and striking them with a stick, Teiresias is transformed from a man to a woman. Once the gesture is repeated, the transformation is cancelled. Then Zeus and Hera summon him to resolve an argument that has broken out between them about who, male or female, has greater enjoyment during sexual relations, having had the experience in both sexes. Teiresias replies that sexual pleasure is much more intense for the woman, and Hera punishes him with blindness. By way of compensation, Zeus gives him the faculty of divination by way of a gift (Ovid *Metamorphoses* III 324 ff).[6]

In the second version of the myth Teiresias, having seen Athena bathing nude, comes away blinded; by the intervention of Teiresias' mother Chariclo, Athena bestows on him the faculty of divination, a stick and the power to preserve his reason even after death (Callimachus *Hymns* V).

What appears to be the dominant factor in these two myths is their common reference to a sexual matrix as the cause of blindness. The setting is frivolous compared to the content of the myths. But that makes the content itself all the more enigmatic.

In both myths Teiresias is punished. *Blindness* is thus a punishment. But the punishment is not due to an actual sin. It is 'fate' (*tyche*) that leads the soothsayer towards the act for which he will be punished. The extent of this fate lies in the compensation he receives for his punishment: second sight, *oran to aphanes* (seeing the invisible).

Second sight is too great a gift for men. They cannot simultaneously endure the sight of that which is apparent (*to pros posi*) and that which is hidden (*to aphanes*). The initiate 'closes his eyes' in order to 'see', and the fate of the sages is the same. (Plato will recall this when he speaks of Thales who, having fallen into a well while looking at the stars, was reproached by a slave-girl who said "that he was passionate about knowing the things of heaven, but forgot what was nearby."[7])

In this respect the fate of Oedipus is similar to that of Teiresias. His blinding is the punishment for a sin decreed by Tyche. Oedipus' act itself also contains a sexual matrix; he has lain with his own mother, producing sons who were brothers (after killing his father). In fact he declares himself to be a "child of Fortune."(1 1080) Once blind, on the outskirts of the city, he will regain the venerability appropriate to higher beings.

Usually Teiresias and Oedipus are contrasted as mouthpieces for two different truths: the archaic, oracular, Apolline truth of the former, and the rational and scientific truth of the latter, to be attained by degrees. In fact, the fates of the two characters share one common feature. Their path through the darkness in search of an invisible light, their constant hesitation between darkness and light. It is in this dazzling contrast that the highest notes of the tragedy sound. Darkness and light, blinding: words that call to mind an unwanted sin, the content of which is something obscurely sexual, a game of the gods, a terrible weight for men.

A trace of this mystery appears in the myth of the origins of the world. The *diakosmesis* begins in Chaos and Night, with a wedding: that of *Gaia* and *Ouranos*, Earth and Heaven. In a timeless embrace they produce, amongst others *Kronos*. Spelt with '*ch*', *Chronos* means Time.

"But those who were born from Gaia and Ouranos were the most terrible of children and were hated by their own father from the first. And he hid them all away in Gaia's breast as soon as each was born, and would not allow them to come to light: and Ouranos rejoiced in his evil doing. But prodigious Gaia groaned within, being tight-pressed inside, and devised a deceitful and evil stratagem. She made the element of grey flint and shaped a great reaping-hook, and told her plan to her dear sons, cheering them, while she was vexed in her heart: 'My children, begotten by a sinful father, if you will obey me, we shall punish your father's vile outrage; for he it was who first thought of doing shameful things.' Thus she spoke, but fear seized them all, and none of them uttered a word. But great Kronos the wily replied thus to his dear mother: 'Mother, I will undertake to do this deed, I promise, for I care not our execrable father, for he was first to do shameful things.' Thus he spoke, and mighty Gaia was delighted. Then she hid him in ambush, and handed him the huge sickle with its sharp teeth, and explained the deception. Great Ouranos came, bringing night with him, and wishing for love he lay down and spread himself all over Gaia; but from his hiding-place, his son reached out with his left hand and with his right he took the terrible great sickle with its sharp teeth, and quickly cut off his father's genitals, and flung them behind him to fly where they might. They did not escape his hand in vain, for all the drops of blood that flew off were received by Gaia." (Hesiod *Theogony* 1 154 ff)

The series of births that populates the world of mortals and immortals is thus marked at the outset by a deception of a sexual nature. Through the act of castration, the Earth detaches herself with the help of Kronos (Time) from the embrace of Heaven. And it is from this bloody deed that the possibility of a world is born for mortals. Inscribed within the *diakosmesis* dictated by the myth, they seem to go back over, as if through a mirror, the painful separation of Earth and Sky and the beginning of Time.

Kronos' act occurs at night. The weapon, a sharp-toothed sickle, "is the image of that moon first emerging from the deepest darkness of night".[8] The moon, the glass mirror of the sun's light, is bound to mortals. Its cycles mark the path of time.

It would therefore appear that man, if he is to take this path through the vision of what is, was and shall be, must pay a price. His wisdom, if he is to grasp the light, must grope in the dark. The fate of Oedipus and Teiresias is the fate of him who "sees what is invisible".

A fragment of Anaximander (B1) says: "The source from which existing things derive their existence is also that to which they return at their destruction, according to necessity; for they give justice and make reparation to one another for their injustice, according to the arrangement of Time."

This seems to allude to a primal distinction: that between *ex on* (the things from which) and *ta onta* (the things that are). The things that are, are manifested by things. But what presence is indicated by *ex on*?

The fragment says: "they mete out punishment and make reparation to one another for their injustice." Here emerges the tragic sense of Anaximander's text. In it there lies the resonance of an involuntary and primal sin that binds to their birth "the things that are". This unfolds "according to the decree of Time". It thus concerns mortal things.[9]

Once again the allusion seems to be with the relationship between appearance and invisible. The metaphysical explanation of tragedy, this relationship refers back to Creon's words about the Sphinx: 'that which is near' (*to pros posi*) and 'the invisible' (*to aphanes*). The things from which is birth to the things that are constitute the hidden, invisible bottom of the universe. There is a movement: birth, (*genesis*). That movement is tragic.[10]

The one who knows that that which exists is appearance, that there is a tortuous path back towards an invisible origin (*arche*), is the *mantis* (the soothsayer). The etymology of this word is extremely rich. Its roots lie in (*mainomai*), which means 'to be invaded, possessed by the god', but also 'to be mad'. The noun (*mania*) in fact means 'invasion' and madness'. What these words have in common is a movement towards the Open[11]. 'Being invaded' or 'being mad' indicate a 'coming out of'.

In a passage of the *Phaedrus* (244a) Plato says: "It might be said that madness (*mania*) is an evil; now, though, the greatest blessings come to us through madness, as a divine gift."

The sapiential movement from "coming out of oneself" is a gift given to men by the gods. It alone permits the knowledge of what is, was and shall be.[12] Another movement is opposed to it, that of 'comprehending', of 'being in oneself' that Plato calls *sophrosyne* (*Phaedrus* 244d). This word comes from *saos* (healthy) and *phronèo* (I am sane, I think, I understand). The noun *phren* in fact indicates the mind. This movement, for Plato, does not lead to true wisdom, in spite of the opinion of the "moderns" (*Phaedrus* 244c). So he sides with the "ancients" on the side of *mania*.

What is at stake in the "madness/being in oneself" (*mania/sophrosyne*) conflict is the "field of revelation" (*to aletheias pedion*) (*Phaedrus* 248b). In order to grasp the revelation one must be possessed by the gods. But *mania* is an ambiguous gift. While it gives wisdom it can, if left to itself, lose man completely. Its invisible light is the mirror reversal of eternal night. Herein lies its tragic ambiguity.

Its double face has the gaze of the Gorgon. As one takes leave of one's senses, the movement towards being 'filled with god' is only a possibility. Being struck by *mania* constitutes a mortal risk: it means crossing the boundaries of one's own human essence, leaving one's social limits, entering the darkness. So the figures possessing this gift remain on the margins, within an undefined horizon that has opened up between animal and god. Teiresias, Oedipus, Demodocus,[13] Homer: the great sages of ancient Greece have a mark, they are *blind*.

Thus Oedipus welcomes the *mantis* Teiresias: "'Teiresias, you are versed in everything, things teachable and things not to be spoken, things of heaven and things that creep on the earth. You have no eyes but in your mind you know...'" (Sophocles *Oedipus the King* 300 ff) Teiresias' *mania* ploughs heaven and earth, it concerns the expressible and the inexpressible. His gaze, blind to 'that which is near' (*to pros posi*), grasps 'the invisible' (*to aphanes*).

A passage in the *Ancient Medicine* (I), strangely close to these lines of Sophocles, sheds light on the problem. The entirely different context in which it occurs recalls the Platonic polarity of madness/wisdom (*mania/sophrosyne*). Hippocrates says: "So I have deemed that medicine has no need of a new hypothesis, as do things invisible and inexplicable (*ta aphanea te kai aperomena*), about which a hypothesis is required if one undertakes to say anything at all about them—for example, about things in the heavens (*ton meteoron*) or under the earth (*ton upo gên*); if anyone should recognise and state how these things are, it would be clear neither to the speaker himself nor to his listeners whether what he says is true or not, for there is nothing, as there would need to be, that we could refer to which would allow us attain clear knowledge (*eidenai to saphes*)."

Hippocrates is defining the field of a science. The demarcation line cuts out 'invisible things' (*ta aphanea*). Among these, for example, he cites "the things above us" or "below the earth". They are not part of science, in that they lack certainty. Here too, as in the passages from *Oedipus the King* (1 130–131) and the *Phaedrus* (244) what is at stake is the polarity *to pros posi/to aphanes* (visible/invisible), *mania/sophrosyne* (madness/wisdom). But the contents have changed their direction. The objective is no longer 'the field of revelation' (*to aletheias pedion*), but 'certainty' (*to saphes*).[14]

In tragedy, on the other hand, the field of wisdom has not dismissed the *invisible*. The presentation that Oedipus makes of Teiresias covers with the same confidence the field that Hippocrates excludes from his knowledge. The inescapable condition is the *blindness* of the wise man. It makes it possible to grasp invisible things.

This apparent contradiction acquires its tragic light in the subsequent dialogue between Oedipus and Teiresias: "You live always in the night, so you could not hurt me or anyone else who sees the light." (*Oedipus the King* 374–375)

In these words of Oedipus', the opposition is between the one who lives in the 'night' and the one who 'sees the light'. The two worlds are held to be incommensurable. He who lives in darkness is not granted contact with him who lives in the vision of present things. The loss of the 'visible': for Oedipus that is the misfortune of the soothsayer.

But the accusation is turned back against him. Teiresias says: "Since you have taunted me with being blind, here is my word for you. You have your eyes but do not see where you are in sin, nor where you live, nor whom you live with." (*Oedipus the King* 412–414) Two words of similar meaning (*derkomai* and *blepo*) are opposed to one another.

Oedipus sees and does not see at the same time. He sees 'that which is near' (*to pros posi*), but the invisible (*to aphanes*) eludes him. Blind Teiresias is the harbinger of this tragic prophecy. The realm of darkness and the realm of light are opposed and then converge. But Oedipus will only be able to see when, at the end of the tragedy, he blinds himself with his own hands. Only then, when he says, "O light, let me see you for this last time!"

Oedipus' path, which measures the distance between visible and invisible, is a path in which darkness and light mark out the risk of knowledge. This risk is not a choice. It is inscribed within the workings of fate.

Rilke says: "As Nature gives the creatures over to the risk of dull desire and shelters none in particular, in soil or bough, so we too are not more dear to the utmost depth of our being; it risks us. Only that we, still more than plant or animal, go with this risk, will it; sometimes even risk more (and not from self-interest) than life itself does; by a breath risk more… This fashions us, outside of all defence, a safebeing, there were the gravity of the

The riddle of the Sphinx

pure forces takes effect; what saves us at last is our defencelessness and that seeing it threaten we turned it into the Open in order, somewhere, in the widest Compass, where Law touches us, to say yes to it."[15]

Man, unlike animals and gods, is not 'especially dear'. The child of *Tyche*, he is by essence 'daring'. He can raise himself to heaven or creep on the earth: 'for a breath' he dares. His fate is marked: he is the one who sees, behind things themselves, the foundation.

It is not out of violence that Oedipus blinds himself. The violence inherent in the gesture blurs its meaning. It is a gesture of submission: when 'the law touches us', Oedipus is 'without protection'. The challenge made to his fate is itself part of his fate. Teiresias knows this.

Grasping 'the invisible' is a matter of a 'breath', but that breath blinds, it transforms values. Light becomes darkness, and the truth shines in the night. Oedipus and Teiresias have no fixed and defined essence. They are in the 'Open'. This lack of limits is at the root of their tragic nature.

The fate of mortals is to "bring the invisible to light". Anyone who stops at "seeing what is near" risks nothing, but will not reach "the field of revelation".

Aeschylus says: "The sleeping mind shines with eyes, while by day it is the fate of mortals to see nothing that lies in front of them." (*Eumenides* 104 ff)

THE INVISIBLE CONNECTION

THE DARK THINKER of Ephesus privileges the invisible: "The invisible connection is stronger than the visible." (*Armonie aphanes phaneres kresson*) (B54) This begins with the *logos*, the word.

Heraclitus' word is twofold. Like Apollo's, "it neither speaks nor conceals, but indicates." (B93). Insofar as it 'indicates', the word is constituted as a fundamental movement: it reveals that which is hidden. But precisely because it is not stuck within itself, it is twofold. Hence its enormous power.

The Sophist Gorgias says (B11): "Speech (*logos*) is a great power, which achieves the most divine works by means of the smallest and least visible form."[1] It deceives the soul. It is thus connected with the soul.

Its twofold nature is already to be found in Hesiod (*Theogony* 27–28). The Muses who reveal to him the mysteries of the Theogony do not always tell the truth. Sometimes, in order to deceive, they announce falsehoods to mortals. The power of the word strikes at a distance.[2]

The god of the oblique word is Apollo. ("*Loxìas* means The Oblique, l'Oblique, if we interpret it based on the epithet *loxòs*.")[3] The etymology of *apollymi*, on the other hand, has the meaning of "he who destroys totally".[4] While in the *Iliad* he is presented as the one who slaughters with the bow, speaking through the mouth of the oracle he expresses the killing riddle.

The word that 'indicates' without 'speaking' is not an innocent word. Its ambiguity leads to death. But in order to know, the word is necessary.

Odysseus certainly knew this, when he demanded to be tied to the mast of the ship as they approached the Sirens, lest he be dragged in by their song. They said: "Draw near, renowned Odysseus, man of many tales, great glory of the Achaeans, and bring your ship to rest that you may hear our voices. No one ever sailed his black ship past this spot without listening to the honeyed tones that flow from our lips; and none who has listened has not been filled with joy and gone on his way a wiser man. For we know all that on the broad plain of Troy the Argives and Trojans suffered by the will of the gods, and we know all that happens in this fruitful world." (*Od.* XII 184 ff)

What is at stake is the risk of knowledge. In the first evidence of Greek thought concerning the value of knowledge for men, it presents itself as *deception*. Circe had in fact warned Odysseus: "First you will come to the Sirens, who bewitch all those who come near them. If anyone draws in unawares and hears the Sirens' voices, no homecoming will he have; his wife and children will never welcome him home again. For with their high clear song the Sirens enchant him, as they sit there in a meadow piled high with the mouldering skeletons of men, the flesh still rotting from the bones." (*Od.* XII 39 ff)[5]

The song of the Sirens is a sapiential song. But anyone who listens to the voice of knowledge dies. The torment suggested by Circe to Odysseus is that of listening, bound, to that voice. While his companions, who have to row, wear wax plugs in their ears to keep from being distracted from their activity, Odysseus feels the weight of his decision: life versus wisdom.

Odysseus' choice of life dismisses Homeric pessimism concerning mortals, but does not remove the problem. The crossroads that Odysseus reaches is a crossroads that is inevitable for man, it concerns the very essence of the word. The invisible ground of the world is that which expresses it as a risk.

If the *logos* stopped at the visible, the Sirens would have no reason to exist.

The sage of Ephesus says (B56): "With regard to the knowledge of visible things, men are deceived just as was Homer, the wisest of all the Hellenes. For he too was deceived by boys killing lice, who said: 'What we have seen and grasped, that we leave behind; but what we have not seen and have not grasped, that we bring.'" It is a fragment divided into two parts. The first is the Heraclitean inversion of the second, concerning the death of Homer.

It is related that Homer, sitting on a rock on the island of Io, upon meeting some fishermen asked them if they had caught anything. They, alluding with a riddle to lice, replied: "What we saw and grasped, that we leave behind; but what we did not see and did not grasp, that we bring." Homer, unable to solve the riddle, died of discouragement.[6]

Heraclitus does not mention the end of the story. The fact that Homer, the "wisest of all the Greeks", really died was probably a detail of little relevance to him. What counts is the shortcoming of the sage, which recalls to Heraclitus' sarcasm the shortcoming of mortals with regard to that which is visible.

Just as Homer encountered the fishermen's riddle, so in the riddle mortals collide with visible things. Homer was *blind*. Being unable to see things that were manifest, he knew invisible things. But his wisdom turned against him. He missed the dark word, the realm of deception.

In the same way, mortals are deceived about what is visible. They think it is real. They do not know that the bottom of things is concealed. Like Odysseus, they choose appearance over life, but do not realise that they are thus defeated by the riddle of knowledge. The word is not innocent, it kills.

"The invisible connection is stronger than the visible one": the perspective of depth is the dimension of Heraclitean wisdom. And in the heart of the abyss he perceives the word. That is why it acquires a twofold richness. He does not stop in the face of the problem of the word either "legally" or "naturally": the movement of the word is the same as that of "nature". Like nature, it "likes to hide" (B123).

The 'invisible connection' is revealed by the word. One has to know how to grasp that which it 'indicates' but does not 'speak'. Anyone stopping at what it says grasps only the 'visible connection'. This connection is a connection of opposites: darkness and light, life and death, mortals and immortals, night and day, waking and sleeping. Anyone who, like Hesiod, fails to recognise that day and night are a single thing (B57) is in error.

Heraclitus' perspective is in the depth, his *logos* is bound to the soul. The word deceives the soul, Gorgias will say. For the sage of Ephesus, "you could not by your going find the ends of the soul, so deep is its word" (B45).

The word is connatural with the soul. Its ends seem to have the same depth as the *logos*. Both are unreachable. But what essence does the soul have for the sage of Ephesus if Aristotle (*On the Soul* 405a) attributes to him the definition of 'origin' (*arche*), as "the warm exhalation of which everything else is composed"?

The soul, in the fragments of Heraclitus, is never opposed to the body. There is no indication of an interior dimension. The external-internal polarity is not primal: so it is of no interest to his thought.[7]

The soul is linked to the abyss (*bathos*) and the word (*logos*). This is "the Open"[8] which opens mortals to the world, but does not belong to them. We experience the death of the soul as the soul experiences our death (B77). The fate of the soul and that of man are the same. Mirrored in the depth of the soul is that 'invisible connection' which binds to itself the opposites of the visible.

The vertigo that we feel when thinking is, for Heraclitus, the measure of that which is by its essence deep: the soul. But mortals cannot grasp what is deep: its boundaries are unreachable. They can only name it. In its twofold nature the world maintains the depth of that which is deep.

Neither does this belong to man. To translate *logos* as 'language' and make it an instrument of knowledge is to misunderstand Heraclitean thought[9]. The *logos* is revealed to man. His task is to listen to it (B50). But "Concerning the word (*logos*), which is eternal, men are without understanding. For though all things come into being in accordance with this Law, men seem as if they had never met with it" (B1).

Listening to the Word means understanding what it 'indicates' and does not 'say': the invisible connection. But there is also a 'visible connection'. For Heraclitus it is of little value. In his fragments Heraclitus in fact speaks of two *logoi*: one is "private", the other "common". "Therefore we must follow that which is common ... But although the Word (*logos*) is universal, the majority live as though they had understanding peculiar to themselves." (B2) "The thinking faculty is common to all." (B113)

The obscurity of Heraclitus' thought reaches three levels. On the first, the soul can be moist or dry. For that reason it is death to become water (B36), while the "dry soul is the wisest and the best" (B118). On the second level the word can be "private" or "common". On the third level the connection can be visible or invisible.

On one side there is the dry soul, from the bottom of which there springs a "common word", which grasps the invisible connection of things. On the other there is the moist soul, to which belongs a 'private word', which stops at the visible connection of things.

There is nothing psychological about this immersion in the depths. It concerns the fate of mortals. It is they who listen to the word that indicates. The two possibilities are intrinsic to their fate.

The connection implicit in the word is the connection of opposites: darkness and light, life and death, mortals and immortals, night and day, waking and sleeping. These opposites do not align themselves with one side or another, in that they are a single thing. "The beginning and the end are common in the circumference of the circle" (B103). Opposites are connatural with man. With them, he reaches a crossroads. Man cannot do without sleep, darkness, death. He is alone among living creatures in moving in the uneasy place between night and light.[10] The contradiction lies in his being held in light, haloed with darkness.

He may be in error. Deceived by the word, the invisible connection escapes him. But it is up to him to grasp what it indicates.

Man is a mortal being. The immortal being becomes the other pole of the relationship. "Mortal immortals, immortal mortals

The song of the sirens

... living their death, and dying their life" (B62). The immortals are immortal by virtue of the fact that a being exists which essentially dies. In that sense they live his death. Immortality does not exist in an absolute sense. If men did not exist, the gods would not exist.

Man's fate lies in his own hands. The crossroads that he reaches is not the work of the gods. It concerns "a very invisible body", the word. But "if one does not hope the unhoped-for, one will not find it, since there is no track leading to it and no path (*aporon*)" (B18).

This fragment clarifies the one about the soul (B45): "You could not in your going find the ends of the soul", because thought is the thought of the unhoped-for, which is by its essence impossible to find and 'trail-less' (*aporos*). Entering the 'deep' (*bathys*) means abandoning every 'path' (*odos*), every 'trail' (*poros*), to accept that which is 'trail-less' (*aporos*). The road is for those in search of a *logos* that 'speaks', but it is a 'private' road that grasps a 'visible connection'.

The wise man, on the other hand, is he who forgets "which way the road leads" (B71).[11] He listens to the word that indicates, he knows is *to bathos*, the abyss. This does not exclude a fundamental pessimism: "All that we see when wakened is death, even as all we see while slumbering is sleep" (B21). On the 'trackless' path, darkness predominates. There is no certainty in *revelation*.

"In the night, a man kindles a light because his sight is quenched" (B26). Even *blind*, man can make light. This possibility granted to him is his only strength. To shed light on the 'invisible connection'. For that reason it is necessary to listen to the word that issues from the soul. The twofold word, which indicates but does not speak.

THE GIFT
OF MNEMOSYNE

E<small>PIMENIDES THE CRETAN</small> "used not to prophesy about the future but about things in the past which were invisible" (B4).[1]

What relationship pertains between 'the past' (*ta gegonota*) and 'the invisible' (*to adelon*) the passage in Aristotle (*Rhetoric* 1418a 21–25) does not say. But a clue does come in the figure of Epimenides. He was held to be "dear to the gods, and endowed with a mystical and heaven-sent wisdom in religious matters" (A4).[2] This reputation also came to him through a myth concerning his life: it said that "lying at midday in the cavern of Dietaean Jupiter, in a profound sleep for many years, he saw the gods, and the words of the gods, and Revelation (*Aletheia*) and Justice (*Dike*)" (B14).[3]

He was one of those sages who still had dealings with the gods. His sleep, which had lasted several decades, had allowed him to see that which is not granted to mortals: *Aletheia* and *Dike*. Diogenes Laertius relates that Epimenides afterwards "got up and went in search of the sheep, thinking he had been asleep only a short time. And when he could not find it, he came to the farm, and found everything changed and another owner in possession. Then he went back to the town in utter perplexity; and there, on entering his own house, he fell in with people who wanted to know who he was. At length he found his younger brother, now an old man, and learnt the truth from him."[4]

The contrast that emerges from this tale concerns time. What Epimenides grasped in his sleep is a dazzling truth measured in an immediate duration. For mortals, a long time has passed. There is no time in dealing with the gods. Or rather, there is no passing of time.

What Epimenides reveals to men after his sleep concerns "divine things". Aristotle says: "Things past and invisible." These terms refer to men.

There is a goddess, named for the first time in Hesiod's *Theogony*, with a very prominent function in Greek thought. Her name is *Mnemosyne* (Memory). Having spent nine nights with Zeus, she gave birth to the Muses, "oblivion of ills and respite from cares". (*Theogony* 55–56)

But the function of the Muses is not solely a comforting one. They sing of "things of the future and things that were before". (*Theogony* 38) They are thus custodians of knowledge and at the same time they establish a link between the poet and memory.

What is being celebrated here is not the knowledge of the future, which is a matter for the soothsayer, but that of the past. Plato says: "The *mania* that comes from the Muses, having entered a pure and tender soul, rousing it to a frenzy in lyric and other forms of poetry, glorifying the infinite works of the past, educates later generations. But the man who reaches the gates of poetry without the madness of the Muses, convinced that skill will make him a good poet, will be an unfulfilled poet, and the poetry of the sane man will be eclipsed by those who are prey to madness." (*Phaedrus* 245a)

'Madness', and not 'wisdom', is thus also a necessity for the celebration of the past. If one is not possessed by the gods, all creative effort is futile. For that reason the bard and the diviner are similar figures. They share "the same gift of 'second sight'", a privilege for which they have had to pay with their vision. They are blind in the light of day, but they can see what is invisible.[5] The power invested in them is strong. They know.

It appears, however, that in Greece the custodians of what has past have been more fortunate than the soothsayers. In the *polis* the soothsayers' role has been reduced to the minimum. Having become mere charlatans, they have lost all credibility. The divination of the past, on the other hand, was a less prodigious feat, but just as complex.

For us, the past is History, a sequence of events in time in which chance is interwoven with the will of men. It is thus at once something extremely concrete and remote. What is past allows us to understand, as a causal factor, the complexity of the present.

For the Greeks, the past was the *arche*, the source, the beginning, that to which one had to return every time. This was not the series of events preceding the present, in that time was not historical time.[6] Each new world was an origin.[7] The past was myth. The essence of the cosmos was its past. Myth, unlike history, is intangible and close. The past lies within the present. But it is grasped only by those possessed by the gods. Mortals thus essentially seem to be excluded from access to two dimensions of time: what has been, and what will be.

Knowing the past is possible, at the cost of the visible: the present. Returning to the source, seeing that from which mortals are excluded. "In moving away from the present we are only leaving the visible world. We step outside our own human universe and discover behind it other regions of being, other cosmic levels normally inaccessible to us. Beneath is the infernal world with all its inhabitants, above the world of Olympian gods. The 'past' is an integral part of the cosmos. To explore it is to discover what is hidden in the depths of being. History as celebrated by Mnemosyne is a deciphering of the invisible, a geography of the supernatural."[8]

Stepping sideways from the visible world—that is the recurrent theme of Greek wisdom. To grasp what has been, you must listen to the word of a goddess, Mnemosyne. She does not belong to mortals. She allows those who are prey to madness to revive themselves with her song, in which the past is celebrated. It comes closer, breaking through the barrier that separates it from the present.

Epimenides' vision becomes clear: he has seen *Aletheia*, Revelation. 'What has been' concerns the truth. And for the Greeks the truth lies in the past in that the past, as *arche*, is the foundation.[9] The source founds. Return to the source unfolds the revelation of what has been. And that, projecting itself into the future, founds what is.

In the Greek conception of time the past constitutes the originary time to which, through Memory, the goddess, we must always return. The idea of 'progress' was unknown to the Greeks.[10] For their thought, the salient events had already happened, the age of gold was over. The progressive remoteness of men from the gods, through a sequence of differences, appears as the increasingly difficult recovery of originary time.

The relationship between the visible and the invisible thus takes its place within the structure of time. The pessimism of the Greeks concerns the time of mortals. The decline of the age of gold marks the progressive impoverishment of the present. And it is within this temporal dimension that the boundaries for the visible are set. The visible, insofar as it is present, thins out over time to make more and more space for the invisible.

The gaze of anyone who, in the present, possessed by god, studies the past, is manifested as immersion in the *invisible*.

The face of the Gorgon

The connection between what has been and the invisible is reinforced in the second dimension of the reign of Mnemosyne: the beyond. This is the dominion of Aides.[11] His realm is that of the dead.

Homer's interpretation of this figure conceals its unfathomable size. The vividly concrete nature of the place, the terrible figure that dominates it, are based on a conception of the universe in which dealings between men and gods are taken as a fact, and the realm of the dead becomes the shadow side of that of the living, whose lord is Zeus. The dead are with the dead, without any positive or negative influence on the living. And Aides appears as the nocturnal face of the lord of Olympus.

One hint seems to interrupt this certainty of colours: in book V of the *Iliad* (l. 845), Athena dons "The Helmet of Hades", to become invisible to a god.[12] The most characteristic quality of Aides shines through. His power concerns the invisible.

In vase paintings he is shown with his face turned back to front. His face could not be looked upon. "No gaze, only the voice was permitted in the Realm of the Dead."[13] When sacrifices were made to Hades, the head had to be turned backwards, as if to repeat in a ritual mirror-image the invisibility of the god.

This gesture of averting the gaze has a peculiar affinity with the attitude of the initiate: closing the eyes. But it is not only an apparent similarity. The sapiential journey that the initiate takes in the Mysteries from darkness to invisible light[14] has the characteristics of a *nekyia* (descent to hell).

Moreover, the eyes and mouth of the dying are closed. The ghosts that populate the house of Aides cannot see. The light in their eyes is extinguished. This does not have a purely negative significance. Like the soothsayer, like the bard, like the initiate, he who has closed his eyes is in contact with the invisible.

The descent into Hades thus has a value that is sapiential as well as ritual. Rohde points out that moral connotations are absent from the Greek conception of the beyond.[15] The only distinction, even in Homer's time, was that between initiates and non-initiates. "The initiated were promised a blessed life hereafter; a gloomy fate awaited the uninitiated. The difference was not made by goodness or badness: 'Pataikon the thief will have a better fate after his death because he has been initiated at Eleusis than Agesilaos or Epameinondas' sneered Diogenes the Cynic. Not political or moral worth but 'spiritual' merit alone is decisive."[16]

The initiate is he who has access to Hades even before his death. So rather than seeing this privilege as a religious fact that is ritual in character, as Rohde does, I see it as a sapiential problem. The journey to Hades, with the gaze turned backwards, concerns knowledge.

Odysseus comes to know, in the house of Aides, from the soothsayer Tiresias, what fate awaits him (*Od.* XI 90ff). And the same thing happens to Orpheus. Having descended to the underworld to find his wife Eurydice, he transgresses the god's rules and turns his gaze towards her face before he has left the gates of Hades. Eurydice disappears. The face of the dead cannot be seen by the living. But Orpheus' journey to the depths has not been a love story. Hidden behind the appearance there lies the true significance of Orpheus' *nekyia*. In contact with Aides and Persephone, he has travelled a path of wisdom. The revelations that he will make when he returns among the living concerning the origins of things and gods[17], the Mysteries that he will celebrate, are the fruit of this "immersion in the invisible".

Orpheus is a son of the Muse Calliope. He thus has connections with Mnemosyne. In his journey to the houses of Aides the appeal to that which has been is bound in unity with the 'invisible things'. The inscription on a gold leaf commemorating Orpheus' journey reads: "This grave is sacred to Mnemosyne. When your time comes to die, you will go to the well-built houses of Aides: there on the right is a fountain, and beside it a straight white cypress; descending there the souls of the dead cool themselves. Do not go too near that fountain; but before it you will find cold water that runs from the marsh of Mnemosyne; and above it are the guardians, who will ask you in the depths of their heart what you seek in the darkness of ruinous Hades. Tell them: I am the sun of the Earth and the starry Sky, I am dying of thirst; give me cold water that runs from the marsh of Mnemosyne. And truly they will show you kindness at the will of the king of the underworld; and truly they will let you drink from the marsh of Mnemosyne, and in the end you will travel far, along the sacred way walked also by the other glorious initiates and those possessed by Dionysus."[18]

In the houses of Aides there is a spring: it belongs to the goddess Mnemosyne. Drinking from it enables one to take a long journey, like that of the initiates. Along that path he who has drunk grasps what lies behind things, behind the appearance of the world. In the pessimism of a thought which identifies a purely illusory quality in the visible, the spring of Mnemosyne constitutes the clue to the grasping of the *arche*, the invisible foundation.[19]

But there is another spring in the houses of Aides: that of Forgetting (*Lethe*). He who drinks from it forgets what has been, the *arche*, the invisible, to let pass only that which is present, the time of life without return.

Lethe is a goddess opposed to Mnemosyne. Her power concerns present time, within which the visible is arranged. He who is possessed by Lethe is not prey to madness, but his gaze does not grasp that which lies behind things. But this opposition is not a moral one. Men live between Memory and Forgetting. There is no possibility of erasing either pole. As mortals, they need forgetting in order to live.[20]

The myth of the two springs also relates to the predestination and transmigration of souls. Anyone who drinks from Mnemosyne halts his cycle, thus reaching the end of his sapiential journey. He who drinks from Lethe will return to live in this illusory world, which is the only world for mortals in any case. The fact that revelation (*aletheia*, truth) does not live there is mortals' tragic fate.

To forget in order to live. But for the Greeks to remember is to know. To know is thus to die. The sapiential journey is a journey towards death. Suppressing present time in order to grasp the originary dimension of time, which is the *arche*, the fount of wisdom, the invisible source, means overcoming the hiatus that separates what is visible, illusory, from what is invisible.

Moreover, remembering implies forgetting. 'Memory' is the "oblivion of ills". (Hesiod *Theogony* 55) Remembering originary time means forgetting the illusory time of life, it means passing through the gates of Hades. It is a *tragic* tangle. It is the contradiction of a thought that bases in seeing its knowledge and then erases, as pure appearance, the object of that which it sees. It is a thought that looks upon the time of life as a descent into appearance and upon originary time as an increasingly remote trace of the presence of the gods.

The myth of *Phaedrus* (248a-250c) exemplifies this contradiction. The souls of the immortals spin in a circle as they contemplate being. Among the souls of the mortals, on the other hand, "the one that follows god best and has come to resemble him most raises the head of its charioteer into the region outside and is carried round with the revolution, meanwhile being disturbed by its horses and scarcely seeing the things that are." This is the field of revelation (*to aletheias pedion*).

"But when it is unable to follow the god, and fails to behold the truth, and through some ill-hap sinks beneath the double load of forgetfulness and vice," because of this weight it loses its wings and plunges to earth, to be made flesh in a human body.

The fall to earth from the circle of immortal souls, absorbed into the magic of revelation, implies a fall into rectilinear time. Originary, circular time marked out the movement of the celestial procession. The distance between them is vast.

But mortals are granted a human recovery of originary time, the *arche*, the source. Once again this process takes place under the tutelage of the goddess Mnemosyne. Plato says (*Phaedrus* 249c): "Man must understand things according to the so-called Idea (*eidos*), arising from many sensations and being brought into a single one through reason." And he adds: "This is a remembrance of the things which our soul saw once when it travelled in company with a god and from high above saw what we now say is, and raised its head up into what really is."

Revelation is grasped by mortals through the memory of what has been.

"But it is not easy for all souls to gain from earthly things a recollection of that true being, nor for those who had once a brief vision of that reality up there, nor or for those who fall to earth and have the misfortune of being dragged to injustice by certain company, forgetting the sacred things they saw then. Few souls remain who have sufficient memory; and these, when they see some likeness of the things in heaven go into ecstasies." (*Phaedrus* 250a)

Revelation is grasped in the bond that memory forges between the illusory nature of the images of this world and the invisible 'origin', overcoming the distance between the two. A sideways leap from the visible. Possessed by madness, men can drink from the spring of Mnemosyne and grasp that which has been the invisible foundation of things.

This recollection contains a conflict: it ratifies, by suppressing it for a moment, the distance from the origin. Plato calls it "longing for what was before".[21] Man's fate is to grasp truth through a shadow. In order to do this, his gaze must be turned backwards.

Rilke says: "Who has turned us around like this, so that, whatever we do, we are in that posture of someone leaving? Just as, upon the last hill, which shows him his whole valley one last time, he turns, stops, lingers – so we live, forever taking leave."[22]

THE CHARLATANS
OF HEAVEN

IN THE LIVES (NICIAS 23), Plutarch recalls the time when "there was no toleration of naturalists (*physikous*), then also known as charlatans of heaven (*meteoroleschas*), because they reduced the divine to irrational causes, to powers without intention, to necessary conjunctures." To quote Plato, the error of these 'physicists' lay in a defect of vision: "From the evidence of their own eyes they that all the bodies which move across the heavens were mere collections of stone and earth and many other kinds of inanimate matter – inanimate matter which nonetheless initiated a chain of causation responsible for causes of all things in the universe."[1]

This intolerance was not without consequences. Anaxagoras was put on trial for heresy and saved at the last minute by Pericles, Socrates was put to death and the books of Protagoras were burned in the agora.

Independent of the accuracy of the accusations, what matters is their substance: the gaze turned to heaven. Not that this was a new thing (the legend of Thales falling into the well because he was looking at the stars is significant in this respect), it was the way in which it was approached that assumed the status of a revolutionary event. The heavens were not full of gods, but of incandescent masses which were in turn composed according to a necessary law.[2]

What is at stake here is the very interpretation of the visible world. And its vivid formulation is: "Visible existences are a sight of the unseen." (*Opsis adelon ta phainoumena*) (Anaxagoras B21a).

The gap between 'seeing' and 'knowing' is polarised around the 'things of heaven'. The gaze turned upon these is the point at which the tragic dimension of the invisible accumulates. Nature's secret harmony breaks down into a play of cross-references, in which the visible suggests the unknown. Here the depth of the universe is concentrated between the infinitely large and the infinitely small (Anaxagoras B3).

This telescopic recession in both directions, macroscopic and microscopic, is dizzying: the surface of the world is the only tangible sign of a hidden truth. The gaze of the physicists is thus set out as the "manière d'aller du visible à l'invisible"[3]. It becomes a *theorein*.

This word, already used by Aeschylus, is composed of *théa* and *orao* (I see). The former, *théa*, is the look, the appearance in which something shows itself, the view in which it offers itself. It also, however, contains an echo of *theá*, the goddess.[4]

This particular 'seeing', then, contains a displacement. Its heuristic force intensifies in the effort to reach the references hidden behind the surface of things, and at the same time the divine is condensed into *theorein*, leaving heaven free.

The journey from the visible to the invisible is thus a 'theoretical' one. The accusation of atheism bears out its revolutionary force. At the moment at which the very movement of 'seeing' reveals itself as divine, there is no more space for other gods. "Concerning the gods, I have no means of knowing whether they exist or not or what their nature may be" (Protagoras B4). Their inaccessibility is the only defence against their disappearance.

René Char says: "Supprimer l'éloignement tue. Les dieux ne meurent que d'être parmi nous."[5] The only goddess guiding the path of the *theorein* is the goddess in Parmenides' poem, 'Revelation' (*Aletheia*), who reveals the invisible with her gaze.

For Anaxagoras, this is *nous*. To translate the word as 'intelligence' implies the introduction of spiritualist connotations alien to his thought. What he sees when he studies the heavens is *nous*. "Everything else has a portion of everything, but mind (*nous*) is limitless (*apeiron*) and autonomous, it is mixed with nothing, but is on its own and by itself. ... It is indeed the most refined and the purest of all things, it has full knowledge of everything, and it is extremely powerful. And all things that have souls, both large and small, are ruled by *nous*. And the impulse for the universal rotation comes from *nous* ... and all those things formed by composition and those formed by separation and those that are divided, all were recognised by *nous*, and all those things that were to be and those which are not now, and those which are now, and those which are to be, all were ordered by *nous*, and the rotation that encompasses the stars the sun, the moon, the air and the aether ... nothing is formed or divided from another thing save by *nous*." (B12)

It is clear that, as a doctrine expressed by a physicist, assertions of this kind would have prompted indignation. And their first and greatest enemy was Plato. To grasp behind what is seen an invisible, such as *nous*, implies a perception of things which preserves within them the antinomy of appearance and hiding. In this gaze there is no opposition between matter and spirit, as Plato points out. And his criticism lies specifically in that direction.[6]

Plato posits the Anaxagorean intuition of *nous* as a causal principle, but he rebukes Anaxagoras for what he considers to be an excessively approximate discourse. However, "Once I heard someone reading from a book that he said was by Anaxagoras, saying that it was a mind (*nous*) that was the ordering principle and the cause of everything, and I was cheered by this, and it seemed to me, in my way, that the idea of mind (*nous*) as the cause of everything was perfectly appropriate." (*Phaedo* 97b-c)

"However, my friend, I felt myself falling from that lofty hope and carried further and further away from it, since as I proceeded with my reading I found that the man made no use of *nous* whatsoever, and assigned it no real principle of causality in to the order of the universe, but found causes in air and aether and water and all sorts of nonsense." (*Phaedo* 98b-c). This would indeed "be a very careless way of talking. In fact it would mean being unable to distinguish that the real cause is quite different, and quite different the medium without which the cause can never be a cause." (*Phaedo* 99b)

Plato is not a "charlatan of heaven". For him, there is no question of leaving ambiguously open the space set out between the visible and the invisible. In his thought they become two different worlds, with different laws. They will be called body and soul, sensible and intelligible.

The vision of Anaxagoras, on the other hand, his *theorein*, looks beyond the appearance of phenomena, while taking them as his starting point. The body of mechanisms governing the cosmos is an invisible force at the root of things. Seeing, *theorein*, thus becomes this movement from the visible to the invisible: from the things of heaven to *nous*. The clarity of this heaven is intrinsic to its own heuristic possibility, freely accessible to a gaze which penetrates the visible to look upon what is hidden.

In the *Theogony*, Hesiod relates how the line of the gods split from that of men. In a banquet at Mekone, Prometheus "took a large ox and, having carved it, served it in such a way as to mislead the mind (*noón*) of Zeus. On one side he laid out meat and entrails rich with fat in the hide, hiding it in the ox's stomach, while on the other side he laid out the ox's white bones, which he arranged carefully for a wily trick by covering them in glistening fat." (l. 536–541) The gods, deceived, took the bones and the fat, while men got the better part. But Prometheus' attempt to favour men was unsuccessful. Zeus, having discovered the deception, created an irreducible distance between them.

In the myth, Prometheus carved up an animal, putting himself on the side of men. His skill in making invisible that which, insofar as it can be seen, is available for choice, makes the enterprise feasible. His familiarity with the hidden parts of the animal deceives the gods. But what should really allow men a victory over the gods instead serves to remove them forever.

As a descendant of Prometheus, Anaxagoras performs a gesture in a non-mythological context with a similar meaning. "It is said that once the head of a one-horned ram was brought to Pericles from his place in the country, and that Lampon the soothsayer , when he saw how the horn grew strong and solid from the middle of the forehead, declared that, whereas there were two powerful parties in the city, the party of Thucydides and that of Pericles, mastery would finally devolve upon one man, the one to whom this sign (*to semeion*) had been given. Anaxagoras, however, had the skull cut in two and showed that the brain did not fill the skull, but had drawn together to a point, like an egg, at the particular spot where the root of the horn began." (Plutarch *Pericles* 6 2)

Present at this "theoretical scene" are a "soothsayer" and a "charlatan of heaven". The former, restricting himself to what he sees, does not capture the truth, but utters a fable. The latter, lowering himself from a visible sign into that which is hidden, emerges victorious. Illuminated by "Promethean tradition"[7], Anaxagoras knows the tricks of the visible. Like the chained god, he knows how to look behind things. Along the theoretical path, the 'soothsayer' is no longer possessed by the gods, like the ancient sages. He is only the one who has not understood that his beliefs are mere superstition. But in the context of the episode all of this is possible, because the gods have vanished from heaven. They are no longer a point of reference. Man is alone on earth in search of traces of the *invisible*.

The defect of vision for which Plato will rebuke the naturalists is the 'Promethean' distance that links what is seen to what is hidden. Covering this distance means measuring the heuristic force of their thought. It removes the *mist* that covers the eyes of men.[8] As such, it is once again a revelation. In it, distance is measured by the vision of the *theorein*. This contains a secret similar to the path of the initiate in the darkness of the Mysteries. The initiate, in order to grasp the invisible light of the ritual, had to "close his eyes". Revelation was preceded by immersion in darkness. The veil of appearance was thus concealed in order to shed light on the hidden things.

Through the 'theoretical' gaze, the vision turned upon the invisible brings with it the darkness of appearance. In fact, "of knowledge there are two forms, one genuine and the other dark. To the latter belong all these: sight, hearing, smell, taste, touch. The former is the genuine one and all its objects are hidden." (Democritus B11)

That which concerns visible things is therefore obscure. Appearance, being limited to what can be seen, is blind. It should be seen as a trace of that which is hidden. Herein lies the true

The ghost of Athena

possibility of knowledge. The path towards invisible things is therefore in the darkness of "that which is near".[9]

For that reason "it is recorded in the annals of Greek history that the philosopher Democritus, a man of ancient authority, venerable above others, voluntarily deprived himself of the sight of his eyes, because he believed that the thoughts and reflections of his mind would be more vigorous and exact in contemplating the rational construction of nature if he had freed them from the enticements of sight and the hindrances of the eyes." (A23)

Leaving aside the trustworthiness of this source, Democritus' blindness, whether voluntary or, more likely, natural, since it afflicted him late in life, has a 'theoretical' justification. At close quarters, the episode recalls the figure of the blind seer, even though the context has changed.

The gesture, or event, is a consequence of *theorein*. It is not an eccentric dimension.[10] It is a dimension born from the very rigour of 'contemplating'. The horizon which measures it is that of a gaze that travels the distance from the visible to the invisible: "when others often failed to see what was before their feet, he used to journey on to infinity, stopping at no boundary." (A22)

The gaze of *theorein*, piercing the visible, reaches hidden truths. Aristotle himself was the first to admit that Democritus was the only one to go beyond the surface of things.[11] The magician of Abdera maintained that between 'the apparent" and "invisible things" there was a distance that obliged one to immerse oneself in the abyss. "Revelation is in the depths (*en bytho gar Aletheia*)." (B117)

His *blindness* constitutes the symbolic representation of this journey into the depths. The 'invisible things' interwoven with the visible, however, are not something unthinkable, divine. They are, in fact, the only thing worthy of contemplation: "By convention sweet, by convention bitter, by convention hot, by convention colour: but in reality atoms and void." (B9)

The 'invisible things' are thus precise figures: bodies so small that they cannot be seen, and that in an infinite quantity compose the universe. All that we see, on the other hand, is deceptive appearance.

But that nexus contains the tragic contrast of *theorein*. The surface of the world, in its manifestly contradictory nature, cannot be avoided. The path that must be travelled in order to grasp what is hidden necessarily passes through it. At the same time the passage from the visible to the invisible is not a safe one. "Therefore Democritus asserts that either nothing is true or that it is invisible to us." (A112)

That which is invisible (the atoms of Democritus, the homeomeries of Anaxagoras) constitutes the perspective – macroscopic and microscopic – of that which is seen. It is the depth of a universe whose surface alone can be grasped. In this sense, the invisible goes in the same direction as the visible.

What will be inconceivable to Aristotle is the 'physicality' of this invisible depth.[12] This is the secret mesh of the universe: 'revelation' (*Aletheia*). The visible is the sign of that mesh. The atom is without perceptual connotations. Its description is possible only in negative terms.

The journey from the visible to the invisible is set out as a "méthodologie scientifique".[13] As with every self-respecting physicist it is a matter of "substituting for a complicated visible a simple invisible".[14] What Plato calls 'defective vision' is in fact the very movement of *theorein*.

The task of mortals is to 'contemplate' through the surface of heaven a hidden universe. For that reason, in opposition to common sense, genuine knowledge is that of hidden things, while obscure, opaque knowledge concerns the apparent world. Seeing is not enough. To know it is necessary to go beyond what is seen, but without going beyond the limits dictated by phenomena.

The pessimism of the 'physicists' in the depreciation of appearance therefore has a heuristic force to it. The revelation of that which is invisible constitutes an infinite but possible quest.

The mesh of infinite quantities that constitutes the false bottom of the universe is a mesh of 'theoretical' possibilities. In order to grasp it, one has to close one's eyes to the reality of phenomena and contemplate them solely as signs of the invisible. The gaze turned towards the sky is the only way to reach this truth. It is a dizzying gaze, because it sees the world as a simple surface. The truth is in the *abyss*. It is up to man to let himself down into it.

THE PARADOX
OF PERCEPTION

The Floods of the Nile

IN THE HISTORIES (II 19) Herodotus relates how, wishing to know the nature of the Nile and above all its floods, he had carried out futile research among the Egyptians. "Some Greeks, wishing to distinguish themselves by their cleverness, have advanced three different explanations about the river" (II 20), two of which he recalled only in order to point out their fallacy.

The most reasonable (even though erroneous) maintains that the Nile comes from melted snow. But this is of course wrong, in that the Nile runs from very hot countries to colder countries. The other explanation says "that the Etesian winds cause the Nile to flood by keeping it from flowing into the sea. However, the Etesian winds often do not blow, and the Nile still floods. Besides, if the Etesian winds were the cause, other rivers facing these winds would surely be affected in the same way as the Nile and even more so, since, being smaller, their current is weaker." (II 20)

The last explanation, the most absurd of all, is the most wonderful to relate. This one says that the Nile "produces these phenomena because it flows from the Ocean, and the Ocean flows all around the world" (II 21). Now this cannot, according to Herodotus, be subject to refutation. The reason is this: the man who told this story "based his tale on the invisible" (*es aphanes ton mython aneneikas*). (II 23)

The discriminating factor that allows the sage of Halicarnassus to refute the first and the second explanation and not the third lies, once again, in the word 'invisible'. The former are refutable in that they posit as a cause for the floods of the Nile 'visible' phenomena: snow and the Etesian winds. The reason why they are in error lies in the link with the effect (in this case the flood of the Nile). The connection between two visible phenomena can thus be mistaken, but for precisely that reason it can be subject to refutation.

The third explanation, on the other hand, is based on an irrefutable presupposition: the existence of the Ocean and its running around the Earth. This formulation is a story that leads beyond observable phenomena. It is an 'invisible' fact. For that reason it is irrefutable. Herodotus, in fact, adds (II 23): "For myself, I have not seen whether there is any river Ocean, but I think that Homer or one of the poets who lived before him invented the name and introduced it into his poem."

In this case, however, the manufacturer of the myth of Ocean is not a poet, but a cartographer who predated Herodotus, Hecataeus of Miletus, the author of a *Periegesis* and a *Mythology*. He, a "traveller and surveyor of the inhabited earth" is held by some modern commentators, with the agreement of some ancient ones, to be an authentic historian, perhaps the very first[1]: Herodotus' position towards him is thus even more interesting, since he is not simply dealing with a fabulist.

The theory of the Ocean is thus displeasing to the sage of Halicarnassus not because there is any shortage of proof of the river's existence. In Herodotus, in fact, the explanation of certain phenomena would be arbitrary. His position is not a 'scientific' one *ante litteram*, but something else.

The appearance of Thetis

The Embroidered Armour

In Book III (chapter 47) of the *Histories* Herodotus relates that the Spartans led an expedition against the Samians, to make them pay for the theft of a bowl that they were supposed to give to Croesus, and a suit of armour that Amasis, king of Egypt, had sent them as a gift. The armour "was made out of linen, and woven with a large number of figures, and embellished with gold and cotton thread. What is especially admirable is that each single thread of the armour, fine though it was, consisted of 360 separate threads, all visible."

This fabulous armour has one particular characteristic: every thread with which it is woven is composed of 360 threads. But what most struck Herodotus' imagination is the 'visibility' of this secret. Its worth lies in the visibility of its threads.

Now, notwithstanding this being one of many such tales of his, I believe that it expresses, hidden within a brilliant image, the way of seeing of the sage of Halicarnassus. His exaltation of the visibility of one thing, which immediately transmutes it into an object of infinite value, does not reside in a casual attribute[2]. The same likely exaggeration of the visibility of the threads (360 for each thread from which the armour is woven multiplies the number to infinity) testifies to the wonder of it.

Generally speaking, the importance of a thing lies in the totality of its appearance. Herodotus in fact asserts: "What I have said has been dictated by my vision and my knowledge and my investigation" (II 99). The description of a thing is thus the direct or indirect vision (from truthful testimonies which are in turn the product of a direct vision) of its visible manifestation.

This alone is important. The invisible, on the other hand, is irrefutable. It constitutes the deception of that which cannot be described. The Ocean is a thing of this kind. Using it to describe the reason for the Nile floods means slipping into the invisible. And, if the embroidered armour is wondrous because it is made up of infinite threads all of which are visible, the Ocean, an invisible river that flows around the earth, is an assertion that provokes laughter[3].

The Dismissal of the Invisible

To know is to see. This conception presents no problems for Herodotus. There is wisdom as far as the eye can see (directly and indirectly). The world is only surface. But the repression of its invisible depth conceals the fear it arouses. The exaltation of the visible thus becomes a flight from the anxiety of the unknown.

Shortly after Herodotus (straddling the V and IV centuries BC), a doctrine in the field of medicine develops in Cos, which takes 'seeing' as its starting point and its goal: that of Hippocrates.[4]

Medicine, like the *Histories* in a sense, is on the fringes of thought. Its place is a sapiential non-place. It is a *techne*, an art whose characteristic is that it coexists with life and death. Its first dimension is the *gaze*. The fates of the sick are woven into it.

"The observing gaze refrains from intervening: it is silent and gestureless. Observation leaves things as they are; there is nothing hidden to it in what is given. The correlative of observation is never the invisible, but always the immediately visible, once one has removed the obstacles erected to reason by theories and to the senses by the imagination."[5] With these words we may summarise Hippocrates' position. His path, in stripping medicine of all religious and dogmatic residues, is formulated in the realm of 'sensation' (*aisthesis*).

Hippocrates says in the *On Ancient Medicine* (I): "So I have deemed that medicine has no need of a new hypothesis, as do things invisible and inexplicable (*ta aphanea te kai aporeomena*), about which a hypothesis is required if one undertakes to say anything at all about them – for example, about things in the heavens or under the earth; if anyone should recognise and state how these things are, it would be clear neither to the speaker himself nor to his listeners whether what he says is true (*alethea*) or not, for there is nothing, as there would need to be, that we could refer to which would allow us to attain clear knowledge (*eidenai to saphes*)."

The medic of Cos could not be clearer on the matter. His declared method delimits a horizon defined by the gaze. Circumscribed within it is everything visible. "Indeed we must seek somehow to attain a certain measure, and yet that measure admits neither number nor weight of any kind by which it might accurately be determined, unless it be the sensation of the body (*tou somatos ten aesthesin*)." (*On Ancient Medicine* IX)

The gaze and the senses thus constitute the practical scope of medicine.[6] Its field of observation lies between the past (*anamnesis*) and the future (*prognosis*). "For the physician, it seems to me, it is an excellent thing to practise prognosis: by foreseeing and foretelling, in the presence of the patient, his present, past and future condition, and analytically describing the things that the patient himself has neglected to do, he will the more readily be believed to understand the situation of the patients, so that they will dare to trust him. And he will be able to plan an excellent treatment if he has foreseen future developments from present ills." (*Book of Prognostics* I)

Within this spatio-temporal ambit, medicine lies between the 'symptom' (*tekmerion*) and the sign (*semeion*)[7]. This oscillation of the visible prompts the secret paradox of the Hippocratic doctrine: the removal of the invisible. The symptom presents itself as the very phenomenality of the illness, its appearance on the surface of the body: to signal its presence, to show the efficacy of the treatment. In the mute dialogue between doctor and patient, the patient constitutes a guarantee of certainty.

As a sign, the *semeion* announces. "Between it and the disease there lies a distance that it cannot cross without accentuating it, for it often appears obliquely and unexpectedly. It offers nothing to knowledge; at most it may outline a recognition."[8] The sign is a 'vision of the invisible'. In the Hippocratic doctrine, however, it reveals only the surface. It refers to nothing but itself or to a future visibility.

The cases quoted in his works all go from phenomenon to phenomenon. The doctor's gaze runs from sign to symptom "in a circle that must not be broken".[9]

This reduction of sign to appearance, while on the one hand it leads to abdication with regard to the invisible on grounds of inexplicability, on the other it recovers it from a *post-mortem* truth. The depths hidden from the doctor's gaze in the course of the illness rise to the surface with the dissection of the corpse. The visible horizon of observation yields diachronically to the subtle difference between the body of the patient and the corpse.

This passage concerns the 'truth' of the treatment. It is a *revelation*. The corporeal surface unveils itself to the doctor's contemplation. What was still hidden in the course of the illness, in that the sign referred solely to itself, becomes manifest in the visible light of dissection. The mystery of this process is that "[t]hat which hides and envelops, the curtain of night over truth, is, paradoxically, life; and death, on the contrary, opens up to the light of day the black coffer of the body."[10]

The beginning of the practice of dissection, inaugurated by Alcmaeon[11], which undergoes an important development with the Hippocratic school, inserts the caesura of death into the visible space of the gaze. The suppressed *invisible* is thus restored on another level, which shifts the visible signs of the prognosis into an unmoving truth.

This earthly process, however, is only possible by erasing all religious and divine residues from the horizon of observation. The reclusion of "the things above us and the things under the ground", and thus of the invisible things, in the realm of uncertainty and unthinkability is a decisive gesture. It reclaims for man a space in which certainty can be reached on earthly paths. At the same time it denies him the intervention of the gods.

Alcmaeon had already written (B1) that "concerning things unseen (as) concerning things mortal, the gods have certainty, whereas to us as men conjecture alone is possible". His position therefore warned of the very risk of knowledge within the man-god-invisible nexus. But, reserving 'total vision' for the gods, he bestowed upon the heuristic project of men the shadow of a religious pessimism.

Hippocrates frees himself from all this. All illnesses, in fact, are "all divine and all human. Each has a nature and power of its own; none is hopeless or incapable of treatment." (*The Sacred Disease* 21)

Epilepsy (the sacred disease), for example, "is in my opinion no more divine than any other; it has the same nature as other diseases, and the cause that gives rise to individual diseases. And it is curable, no less than other illnesses, unless by long lapse of time it is so deeply ingrained as to be more powerful than the remedies applied to it." (*The Sacred Disease* 5)

Those who, according to Hippocrates, have conferred a sacred character upon the disease are "magicians, purifiers, charlatans and impostors, men who claim to be very devout and to see further than others. Being at a loss, and having no treatment which would help, they concealed and sheltered themselves behind superstition, and called this illness sacred, in order that their utter ignorance might not be manifest ... By speaking and plotting in this way they claim to be able to see more deeply, and deceive men." (*The Sacred Disease* 2–3)

Making the disease divine is thus a way of masking the ignorance of a *blind* gaze. The doctrine of 'sensation' is a doctrine of man for man. The gods have nothing to do with it. The ancient sages, at the moment when they interfere with dogmatism or magic, become for Hippocrates impostors who, with the excuse of being more far-sighted, cannot in reality see any further than what is in front of them.[12]

Divine things are then part of that realm of the *invisible* that medicine seeks to banish. But medicine is situated within that critical line that runs between life and death. The free gaze upon the corpse is heralded as a tragic deception of the repressed invisible.

THE DOUBLE VISION

Amidst the dazzling splendour of Greek thought, two words prompt an 'obscure' interlacement: *eidos* and *aides*. The first is aspect, form, insisting on the theme of appearance, of seeing.[1] The second is the name of a god, Aides, the lord of darkness. With these, Greek thought reaches a point of no return. Here dwell the soul, knowledge, death.

The singer is the last of the sages: the Athenian Plato. One of his dialogues, the *Cratylus*, discusses the origin of names. "And Aides – I imagine most people think that this is a name of the Invisible (*to aides*), so they are afraid and call him Pluto" (403a). In fact, "the name 'Aides' is not at all derived from the invisible (*tou aidous*), but far more likely by knowing (*eidenai*) all fine things, and for that reason he was called Aides by the legislator." (404b)

The secret of this passage lies in a word that is barely uttered: *aides*, "invisible". Plato is the creator of this word.[2] When he speaks of the 'invisible' he speaks of *aides*. The other terms for it, (*aphanes, adelon, aoraton*) are in his view secondary.

The meaning of this choice lies in the passage in the Cratylus. The etymology that Plato finds in *aides* is connected to Hades and to *eidenai*, to knowledge, and thus to 'idea' (*eidos*). The road from Hades to the idea is the crucial nexus of Greek knowledge. This is entrusted by Plato to the word *aides*, invisible.

Again in the *Cratylus* he explains that most people fear Hades "because, once each of us dies, he is always there ... and because the soul goes from him naked of the body, this too they fear" (403b). The error is obvious. Aides is "a perfect sophist and a great benefactor of those near him" (403e). And besides, "he does not wish to be with men who have bodies, but only when the soul is pure of all the evils and desires concerning the body. Do you not think this shows him to be a philosopher, someone who has reflected that he could only restrain them by binding them with the desire for virtue?" (403e-404a). It is for this reason that the etymology of the name Aides allies itself so well with the idea of "knowing all the fine things".

Man's fate seems to approach knowledge only when the soul, stripped of "the body's covering", reaches Hades. "Will anyone who is truly a friend of wisdom, and who holds in his heart the certain faith that he will find that wisdom in its entirety nowhere but in Hades, will he be resentful at dying; and will he not be glad to go there?" (*Phaedo* 68a-b)

In Plato, the soul becomes the very foundation of man. The possibility of its living separately from the body joins in unity with knowledge and with death. Man is the mirror of the world. He divides the creatures, conferring meaning upon them.

"Then do you wish us to posit," Socrates asks Phaedo in one brilliant passage (*Phaedo* 79a-b), "'two forms of beings (*eide ton onton*), the one visible, the other invisible? (*to men oraton, to de aides*)' 'Let's posit those.' 'And that the invisible (*to aides*) is always constant, whereas the visible (*to oraton*) never is?' 'Let's posit that too.' 'Then tell me,' he added, 'we ourselves are part body and part soul, are we not?' 'Exactly so.' 'And to which of these two forms do we say that the body is more similar and more akin?' 'That's clear to anyone: obviously to the visible.' 'And what about the soul? Is it visible or invisible?' 'It's not seen by human beings, at any rate, Socrates.' 'Obviously we refer to things visible and invisible with reference to human nature; did you think we were referring to some other nature?' 'No, human

The eclipse of the sun

nature.' 'What do we say about the soul, then? Is it visible or invisible?' 'It's not visible.' 'So it's invisible?' 'Yes.' 'Then the soul is more similar than body to the invisible, and the body to the visible.' 'That must be so, Socrates.'"

The visible and the invisible are thus the two forms par excellence, in which beings present themselves to mortals. And this is possible for Plato in that man himself is by his essence made up of a visible part (the body) and an invisible one (the soul).

But which are the entities that he posits in this antinomy? The answer of the *Phaedo* is clear: the things that can be grasped only with the mind (*nous*) are invisible, those perceived with the senses (*aesthesis*) are visible.[3]

The revelation (*aletheia*) of the invisible is the truth of mortals. This is possible in that man possesses (or is possessed by) a fragment of it. The journey towards the progressive detachment from the body is the esoteric path into the light of the invisible.

"So the soul, the invisible part of us, which goes to another place of its same nature, meaning its same nobility of origin, pure and invisible—goes to the Invisible (*eis Aidou*) properly so-called—into the presence of the good and the wise god." Once there, "in truth it will be happy, now free of wandering and folly and fears and wild passions, and all the other ills of humanity; and truly, as is said of the *initiates*, it will spend the rest of its time in the company of the gods." (*Phaedo* 80d-81a)

"Closing the eyes." In the Mysteries, the soul's journey towards Hades illuminates, in the passage from life to death, the path of the initiate. The death of the body makes possible the knowledge of the soul.

The visible is the messenger of the *invisible*. It heralds it. Its poverty is the possibility of communicating through a mirror that which cannot be seen. The gaze of mortals, turned backwards, is embodied in this possibility. "The farewell to the things of the world"[4] constitutes the energy required to go beyond appearance. The fragment of invisible light that Plato discovers in man marks its belonging to Hades (as wisdom and death).

The Greek universe thus loses its doubleness. The tragic gulf between 'seeing' and 'knowing' is filled in Platonic philosophy. But at a great cost. Plato no longer believes in the visible origin of wisdom.

In this, Plato has learned in toto, while bitterly criticising it, the lesson of the Sophists. Words speak the world. By changing the meanings of the words, Plato literally changes the world.

The visible origin of wisdom is a myth to him. The soul-image of Homer, who celebrates his senseless death in Hades, is a fairy-tale of the ancients. On the other hand, the tragic assertion of Heraclitus that the ends of the soul are unreachable, is indirectly refuted by Plato. He traces its boundaries very thoroughly in the *Republic* (435b ff).

The soul is the truth of man. The source is Orphic, but the contents are new.[5] The fate of the soul is bound to the invisible. Man is made up of two parts. One, transient and visible, is called body; its organs are the senses, deceptive instruments of knowledge. The other, perennial and invisible, is called soul; its organ is the mind (*nous*), the only valid instrument of knowledge.

Two worlds thus approach man: the sensible and the intelligible. Plato introduces a precise hierarchy. Everything is framed within this vision, everything becomes explicable. The *theoria* (contemplation) of the ancients is subordinated here to a position that begins with man, an onto-gnoseological position.[6] The phrase of Protagoras, "man is the measure of all things" (B1), in spite of the critiques in the *Theaetetus*[7], is fully realised.

The gods are abolished. In Platonic ascesis, forms themselves, things in themselves are enthroned. They are true reality, the only one to be contemplated. The rest is myth. "No external monsters exist," Socrates says. "I have no time for them. What matters to me is the abyss that lies within man, to see if it emerges as a smoking Typhon."[8]

For the first time pessimism about sensation is not a problem. The senses deceive, because they are part of a corruptible being, the body. But there are other organs, based on the soul, which allow true contemplation. The world divided in two removes pessimism.

The Orphic doctrine, stripped of its mysticism, thus serves as the basis for a perfectly structured theory of knowledge. Nothing in the foregoing thought is lost. Even the *nous* (mind) of Anaxagoras finds its place in that order. It is no longer a cosmological figure, worthy of "a charlatan of heavenly matters". This, Plato says, signifies the inability to distinguish means from causes. In fact, Anaxagoras' doctrine of the *nous* is pure materialism as far as he is concerned.

For Plato, the place of the *nous* is not heaven but the soul. *Nous* is an attribute of man. "Heaven is transplanted to earth below."[9] "'And tell me,' Socrates asks, 'of all the things that lie within man, is there anything that rules him apart from the soul, particularly since it has intelligence?'" (*Phaedo* 94b). The answer is negative.

The soul is man's destiny. It alone "is made to look upwards ... by studying the real and the invisible." (*Republic* 529b)

In fact "the wonders of the heavens, since they exist within the visible, must be considered the most true and perfect of the realm to which we belong, but remain inferior to the true ... and these can be perceived with reason and intelligence, not with the eye.' (*Republic* 529c-d). With Plato, *theorein* divides into two movements: one, visible, grasps objects as they manifest themselves, the other, psychical, grasps their truth, which is to say their ideas.

Here once again we have the words *eidos* and *aides*. Two worlds confront one another, the sensible and the intelligible. Man is capable of grasping both with different degrees of knowledge. But why does Plato still speak about visible and invisible? This polarity would at first sight appear to be obsolete in his thought. It is in fact too imprecise. It does not permit deeper gnoseological analyses. And yet he can't do without it.

An explanation for this can be found in a short passage in the *Phaedo*. Plato is criticising Anaxagoras and creates a 'fake' biography of Socrates. '"After this,' he said, 'weary as I was of such investigations, I thought I should take care to ensure that I should not suffer the fate of those who observe and examine the sun during an eclipse: they lose their eyes, if they do not consider the image reflected in water or something of that kind. I too thought that way, and feared that I would blind my soul if I looked directly at things with my eyes and tried to grasp them with each of my senses. And I thought I must take refuge in concepts (*tous logous*), and observe in them the truth of things that are *(ton onton tin aletheian)*'" (*Phaedo* 99d-e)

Socrates is reconstructing the birth of the theory of ideas. And he starts with a clear simile. The sun, if seen directly with the eyes, blinds. To observe it, one must resort to a trick. One must observe its reflected image. In the same way, the things grasped through the senses *blind*. This is to say that the senses cannot endure the sight of them. They are, in fact, deceptive. It then requires an intermediary that can act as an image. This intermediary consists in concepts (*logoi*), a word that Plato will fill with 'idea' (*eide*), meaning, precisely, images.

This seems to contradict his thought. Are ideas not models of things, the true reality? Socrates immediately corrects himself: "Perhaps in a sense my comparison is inappropriate. Because I cannot admit that one who observes things in concepts sees them more in images than those who observe them in facts." (*Phaedo* 99e-100a).

The correction too is clear. But is not entirely satisfactory. Socrates says that the comparison was imprecise, because it is not true in reality that concepts are the reflected image of things, at least not any more than they are reflected through the senses.

In this passage, Plato, theorising ideas, calls them 'images'. Preserving their etymology, he then denies their significance, giving them a different status. But this is no coincidence. The term 'idea' (*eidos*) contains within it both of these poles. It is possible to call them both 'visible' (*oraton*) and 'invisible' (*aides*). In fact, ideas are at the same time 'principally visible' and 'principally invisible'.

The common origin of the words 'Idea' (*Eidos*), 'Hades' (*Aides*), 'know' (*eidenai*), and 'invisible'(*aides*) is thus for Plato a question that concerns the very essence of man. Following the tradition of the ancient sages, for the last sage of Athens too, knowledge calls life into question.

'Knowing' means reaching the place "that is most frightening" (Hades), because for the sages it is unthinkable. "'No earthly poet has ever celebrated that place above the heavens, and nor shall they ever duly do so. But this is the way, for one must be bold enough to tell the truth particularly when speaking of truth itself. In this place dwells that colourless, shapeless and intangible essence, which may be contemplated only by the intellect, the pilot of the soul, that essence which is the source of all true knowledge.'" (*Phaedrus* 247c)

This place is definable only indirectly, through abstractions. And Plato regrets that. If it were in fact visible, the fate of men would be different. "What extraordinary feelings of love it would cause in us if ever thought allowed a clear image of itself to reach our sight." (*Phaedrus* 250d)

The path followed by Plato is a quest for these images. They are 'ideas'. Plato seeks them in the 'intangible', 'formless', 'colourless', 'invisible' Hades. At the very peak of his speculation, in a bid to escape the tragic riddle of the ancient sages, he filled the gap between 'seeing' and 'knowing'. In the division of the world into the 'sensible' and the 'intelligible', a new path opens up, one which leads to the threshold of the twentieth century.

However, Plato knows that this new road is a deception. The interlacement of these words and the very ambiguity of the Idea (full of the visible but extending into the invisible) cannot be erased. In that word Plato dreams of the possibility of seeing the invisible immediately. He incarnates it in the impossible possibility of the soul, supplying it with its own essence.

But at the summit of Greek thought one riddle remains and the circle is closed. Plato, founding Ideas in the Invisible "properly so-called", like Homer, populated Hades with images. And, by bringing a fragment of it to man, he demonstrated yet more violently the bond between knowledge and death.

HERACLES AT THE CROSSROADS

PRODICUS, THE FIFTY-DRACHMA SOPHIST, relates that when Heracles was still a boy, and sitting in a quiet spot, two women came towards him. "One was virtuous in appearance, of noble origin, with a natural complexion, demure of face, modest in bearing and dressed in white, while the other was well-fed to the point of opulence and softness, her face made-up to look too white and too red to be real, her posture too upright to be natural, her eyes wide, and in a robe that revealed as many of her youthful charms as possible" (B2). Heracles, uncertain about which path to take, seems in the end to have chosen the former.

It is perhaps blasphemous to introduce in this way the crossroads that is created in the Greek world after Plato. And it is in fact hard to define which road the face and the gaudy clothes fit, and which they don't. Apparently "the eyes of the body" and "the eyes of the mind" both know which woman to choose even if, behind the surface, things are not so simple.

If we give Plato the choice of Heracles we commit an injustice. Or at least we would need to add his effort to adorn the first woman with the make-up of the other, thus making the vision of the mind more stimulating than that of the body.

If, on the other hand, we give Hippocrates (or those who hide behind his name) the choice of the gaudy woman, we must leave him the merit of having stripped her of all her features, making her as modest as the other.

But it is part of the 'boyish' spirit of the Greeks to hide a possible truth in a playful image. The crossroads they have reached is the fate of their thought. But it is not radical. Plato founded two worlds: the 'visible' one is that of the body; the other, 'invisible', is that of the soul. Subsequent thought, whether accepting them or not, had to come to terms with them.

It is at this crossroads that the path concludes. What lies behind us is a *poikilos mythos*, a motley fable. It tells in fragments the story of a people that had felt the need to "look ... and at the same time to long to go beyond that looking."[1] That longing led to the rediscovery of a word—'invisible'—which in turn marks a journey from Homer to Plato.

Along this path the word 'invisible' has assumed various masks, while still preserving a common foundation. The Gospel of Philip says: "Truth did not come into the world naked, but in symbols and images."[2] The consciousness of the Greeks begins with the opposite presupposition: that which is seen manifests itself with ever greater determination as a mask of truth. Its knowledge is a product of sight, but that is not enough, because the foundation of things remains invisible.

"If we make a concerted effort to stare into the sun and turn away blinded, we have dark-coloured patches before our eyes as what we might call remedies; on the other hand, light-images of the Sophoclean hero—the Apolline mask [meaning appearance—author's note] are the inevitable products of a glance into the terrible depths of nature: light-patches, we might say, to heal the gaze seared by terrible night."[3] It is the dream of this blinding gaze that links these pages about Greek wisdom. A dream that the Greeks have manifested since Homer, and which has never come to an end.

Nietzsche spoke of the discovery of this gaze with reference to the name of a god, Dionysus. The Apolline surface of the Greek world, so celebrated by neo-classicism, had found its abyss.

The women of Heracles

For Nietzsche, only a "pessimism of strength" like that of the Greeks had been able to create the sublime world of tragedy.

Later attempts[4] to bring the Apollo-Dionysus polarity to the heart of Greek thought have remained incomplete, because Nietzsche's fiery images have been translated into an abstract dialectic. Hence the search for a word that would manifest, even for a moment, the consistency of that dream: the word 'invisible'.

Collected within it are the exigencies of the overcoming of appearance. At the same time the gap created between what is seen and what is not provides the possibility of grasping the root of the pessimism of the Greeks. Hence the question of "why the civilisation that founded in what is seen the root of all knowledge maintains that the truth is hidden" has found the possibility of a path.

From the light of Homer to the darkness of the Mysteries, to the riddle of tragedy, to the dazzling word of Heraclitus, we have moved to the contemplation of heaven, to the spring of Memory. In the realm of Plato the path was interrupted. His systematic vision of this dream announces the dazzle of a double vision. Everything that appears on the Greek stage contains that conflict within it.

The call from the invisible to the intelligible (i.e. that which must necessarily be thought) constitutes the possibility of transforming the dream into reality. At the same time the choice of the removal of that dream (undertaken by Hippocrates) represents the confirmation of Platonic thought. Only that which is already divided can be separated.

Greek thought went on to pursue its course in a radicalisation (Scepticism) or in a conciliation (Stoicism, Epicureanism) of both paths. The force of the crossroads, and its dark origin, does not concern only the Greeks. The *Meditations* of Descartes concerning the proof of the existence of the real world, through to the Kantian limits along with the Platonising suggestion (albeit reversed) of the phenomenon-noumenon polarity, have their origins there. The two Platonic worlds of the visible and the invisible are a spectre of this path.

But underlying these 'stellar friendships', there still remains the word 'invisible'. Pascal says: "All this visible world is no more than an imperceptible speck in nature's ample bosom." And he adds: "But to behold another miracle no less astonishing, let him examine the most delicate things he knows … [I]n it I mean to show him a new abyss. I will paint for him not only the visible universe but all the imaginable vastness of nature in the womb of this diminutive atom."[6]

It is the reversal of the myth of the cave.[7] The invisible is constituted as the limit of the visibility of the universe, infinitely reflected as in the mirror in the Flemish painting.[8] It is expressed as the frontier zone between thought and science. Bachelard says, "science concerns only that which is hidden"[9] The programme of science is hence to "substitute a simple invisible for a complicated visible."[10]

Hippocrates' dismissal therefore becomes apparent. The eyes of the body and those of the mind are always in question. Even if the attempt to remain within the field of sensation is taken by positivism and neo-positivism. "In science there are no 'depths'; there is surface everywhere," says the Vienna Circle *Manifesto*.[11] To which we might reply, quoting Hofmannsthal, that the truth is hidden at the surface.[12]

But even the Greeks were aware of the illusory nature of their yearning. The relationship between mortals and immortals decreed the problematic nature of the world. For that reason the sages had been granted the knowledge of the past, the present and the future in exchange for *blindness*. The gap between seeing and knowledge is the root of the tragic nature of their thought. And that gap sounds like a *deception* of the gods.

The gaze of the one who "seeks to know the inmost essence, not the outward show"[13] is a hoax by Mephistopheles.

POSTFACE

NOSTALGIA, or *nostos algos* (desire to return), meant in the metaphorical sense, is, I believe, one of this century's dominant themes.

The disorientation felt by the gaze in the face of the succession of events on the planet has to do with the abyss.

In this unstable progress, the confidence in the precision of the gaze collapses. We look, we are looked at, but we no longer know the reason for it all.

Knowledge as the 'precise' sight of the eye, or in a broader sense the reassuring gaze of the soul, is no longer enough. The gods have left for good, even though the 'wars of religion' have been appearing on the scene more unsettlingly than in the past.

The global multiplication of possibilities of perception is inversely proportional to the 'mist' that covers the clarity of the world.[1]

The negation of the existent, propounded by Adorno[2] at a terribly dark moment in the last century, has an explosive effect even today. In this sense, negation has to do with nostalgia.

The 'no' declared against the rectilinear temporality contained within the myth of progress is connected to the search for a lost Arcadian temporal circularity.[3]

Chekhov's 'To Moscow, to Moscow', with its melancholy ineluctability of an unattainable desire, marks the break with a world that rests its graceful shamelessness on the will to power, to visibility and to the activation of deliberate plans.

Being beside the existent, not being complicit, looking without appropriation, that is *nostalgia*. Which is a fundamental feeling and not a simple collection of reminiscences woven from memory.

Standing 'apart', remaining outside the enchanted circle of power, knowing that beyond the neck of the bottle there may be only the void, but the simulacra of being are not necessarily created by us, taking on the lightness of being. That is what the Greeks can tell us.

Life is based on a deception, it rests on a base of clay. We yearn for immortality, and at the same time we adore only that which is transient in that it is transient. We seek our hopes in the future and look upon the past as a lost and unattainable Eden.

Faith in science, already an oxymoron in itself, to grasp in an ever clearer vision the elementary particles that compose our universe, ourselves included, removes us from a synthetic gaze which for a moment fixes being in its essence.

POSTFACE

The absolute vision of the gods still seems to be mankind's dearest wish. But it is all a deception, because within the very essence of man there lies the invention of that vision, the mirage of the absolute.

This *hubris* of man, this will to power, having set the gods to zero, has lost the right perspective, gaining in omnipotence and losing the true measure of things.

The 'desire to return', or nostalgia, begins with the Greeks, with their 'wandering' in being in search of the truth, illuminated by their sight. Thirst for knowledge, tragic deception, transience of appearance beneath the great dome of time. These themes run down the centuries, changing their appearance but remaining unaltered.

The eye that looks (backwards, Rilke would say) seeks the truth in the zones of the world. We are in time, we are time. We seek to dissipate the 'mist' that enfolds us, we are ourselves that very mist. The invisible is our limit and our goal. And so it was for the Greeks. Time 'ruins' things. And that 'ruin' releases the fascination with an unreachable origin.

This little book recounts a philosophical Grand Tour, grazing in the moorland of ancient Greece. As at Selinunte, at Athens, at Ephesus, the ruins display a brilliant past, equally the Greek words of Homer, Sophocles, Heraclitus, Plato reveal through fragments and suggestions the aporias of our world.

NOTES

Introduction

1. Introduction J Burckhardt, *Storia della civiltà greca*, (Florence, Sansoni, 1955, original ed. 1898–1902), p 706.
2. Cf M Heidegger, *Plato's Doctrine of Truth*, trans Thomas Sheehan, Stanford University Press.
3. G Kittel, *Theological Dictionary of the New Testament*, trans and ed Geoffrey W Bromiley, Michigan 1964, s v: *orao*.
4. Burckhardt, *Storia della civiltà greca*, p 507.
5. E Auerbach, *Mimesis. The Representation of Reality in Western Literature*, Trans Willard R Trask, Princeton, 1953, pp 3–9.
6. This word, in its 'tragic' sense, will be one of this book's fundamental motifs.
7. Aristotle, *Metaphysics*, V, 15, 1021a.
8. The word 'invisible' is represented in the Greek language (until Plato) by three different words: *adelon, aphanes, aoraton*. A fourth word, *aides*, added to Plato's lexicon, will be considered in chapter 8. This multiplicity, rather than stressing translatability of a different kind, constitutes the most dazzling proof of the varied structure of its meaning. The verbs *deloó, phaino, orao* are linked to the bright horizon of the gaze, in terms of its movement as it enters light.
9. P Chantraine, *Dictionnaire étymologique de la langue grecque: histoire des mots*, Paris, Klincksieck, 1968–1977, s v: *a-delon*

10. E Rohde, *Psyche*, Trans. W B Hillis, London 2000 (original edition 1925), p 242: "From such gloomy severity, from the rigid and overpowering dogmatism that a people without imagination had constructed for itself out of religious speculations and visions won by much labour and thought, the Greeks were fortunately preserved by their own genius. Their fancy is a winged god whose nature it is to pass lightly over things – not to fall to earth and there remain ponderously prostrate."

11. In a note of 1953, Pierre Maxime Schuhl wrote that "cette notion des *àdela*, des choses cachées, opposées à celles qui sont patentes, *fanerà*, mérite qu'on s'y arrête, car elle permet de préciser les attitudes d'un certain nombre de philosophes et de savants grecs à l'égard de la connaissance métaphysique, de la science et même de la théologie." [This concept of *adela*, of hidden things, opposed to those which are manifest, *phanera*, is worth lingering over, because it allows us to identify the attitude of a certain number of Greek philosophers and sages concerning metaphysical knowledge and knowledge of science and even of theology.] And he added: "Nous ne donnerons ici qu'une première esquisse de cette recherche qui mériterait, croyons-nous, de plus longs développements." [Here we will only give an initial outline of this research, which would deserve, we maintain, a more lengthy examination.] P M Schuhl, *Adèla*, in: Homo. Etudes philosophiques, Annales publiées par la Faculté des Lettres de Toulouse, 1953, I, pp 86–94.

12. One precedent here that cannot be ignored is Nietzsche's *The Birth of Tragedy*, with its dazzling intuitions about the polarity of the Apolline and the Dionysiac, as well as the subsequent research by Giorgio Colli, a titanic attempt to apply Nietzschean categories to the classical philosophers.

13. Auerbach, *Mimesis*, p 5.

NOTES

14. Plato, *Cratylus*, 403e.
15. Friedrich Nietzsche, *The Birth of Tragedy*, trans Shaun Whiteside, Harmondsworth 1993, p 3. See also the critique of Nietzsche by Ulrich von Wilamowitz-Moellendorff in: *Future Philology!* (trans. Postl, Babich, Schmid, Fordham University 2000, original edition 1872) "Had he known Homer properly, how could he attribute to the Homeric world – a world of youthful freshness, cheerful exuberance in the sweet pleasures of life, refreshingly unspoilt hearts of youthful naturalness, to this springtime of a people who truly dreamt the dream of life in the most beautiful fashion – pessimistic sentimentality, elderly people's yearning for non-existence, and conscious self-deception?"

The Ambiguities of the Visible

1. Auerbach, *Mimesis*, pp 3–7
2. For men, 'hiding' constitutes the equivalent of 'becoming invisible' for a god (cf. the deception of the Trojan horse).
3. I am following the version of *aìzelos*, *ariielos* being a *lectio facilior* (Liddell Scott). "Au sens d'"invisible, disparu' on lit *Il.*, II, 318 *aìzelon* (avec une variante *aìdelos*)." [In the sense of "invisible, vanished" we read at *Il.*, II, 318 *aìzelon* (with a variant, *aìdelos*.)] In a note to the *Iliad* (1883), A. Pierron writes: "Le manuscrit et la plupart des éditions donnent *arìzelon, maxime conspicuum*, mais ce n'est qu'une corruption d'un vrai texte ou une correction faite avec peu de discernement." [The manuscript and most editions give *arìzelon, maxime conspicuum,* but this is only a corruption of the true text or an injudicious correction.]
4. Cf Auerbach, *Mimesis*, pp 3–7xx
5. Thus in book IX of the *Odyssey*, Odysseus introduces himself to Alcinous (ll 19–20): "I am Odysseus, Laertes' son. The whole

147

world speaks of my stratagems, and my fame has reached the heavens."

6. "The gods are terrible if they are seen face to face" (*Il.*, XX, 131).
7. *Il.*, XX, 127–128.
8. This attribute is used only for Penelope's cloth.
9. Calypso "was busy at her loom, shooting her golden shuttle through the warp." (*Od.*, V, 62); Circe was weaving "a web so fine, so soft, and of such dazzling colours as no one but a goddess could weave" (*Od.*, X, 222–223).
10. Thus Odysseus tell the court of Alcinous as he relates the adventure of the Cyclops: "I thought up plan after plan, scheme after scheme" (*Od.*, IX, 422).
11. *Leptòn* is an attribute of the cloths of Circe and Calypso.
12. M Detienne - J-P Vernant, *Cunning Intelligence in Ancient Greece*, trans Janet Lloyd, Chicago 1991 (original edition 1974), p 42. Detienne and Vernant's book made the pages of this chapter possible. Their 'light-hearted' interpretation of *dólos* is still a long way from the 'tragic' interpretation that I have tried to emphasise here.
13. Aeschylus, *Agamemnon*, 1 1382–1383. 3.
14. Cf Lucian, *Dialogue of the Gods*, XVII.
15. M Detienne - J-P Vernant, *Cunning Intelligence in Ancient Greece*, p 296.
16. Cf *Il.*, XIV, 231 ff..
17. *Od.*, XIX, 591 ff.
18. If for the gods, Sleep is a terrible deception in that it substitutes for death, for men it is a pleasant deception because it mitigates the violence of life.
19. *Il.*, XIV, 342–345.
20. *Il.*, I, 359.

NOTES

21. *Il.*, XVI, 790.
22. *Il.*, III, 381.
23. *Il.*, V, 23.
24. *Od.*, VII, 15.
25. *Od.*, XIII, 189 ff.
26. *Il.*, XX, 321 ff.
27. *Il.*, V, 127–128.
28. Chantraine, *Dictionnaire étymologique de la langue grecque: histoire des mots*, s.v. *eìdos*, pp 316–317.
29. *Il.*, XXIII, 94 ff.
30. B Snell, *The Discovery of the Mind in Greek Philosophy and Literature*, trans T G Rosenmeyer, New York, 1982, p 8. Cf also Rohde, *Psyche*, p 5: "The psyche of Homeric belief does not, as might have been supposed, represent what we are accustomed to call 'spirit' as opposed to 'body'."
31. "Then the Cyllenian Hermes summoned the ghosts of the suitors, and in his hand he held the fair golden wand with which he seals men's eyes in sleep or wakes them just as he pleases; with this he roused the ghosts and led them, while they followed whining and gibbering behind him. As bats fly squealing in the hollow of some great cave, when one of them has fallen out of the cluster in which they hang, even so did the ghosts whine and squeal as Hermes the healer of sorrow led them down into the dark dwelling-place of death. When they had passed the waters of Oceanus and the rock Leucas, they came to the gates of the sun and the land of dreams, whereon they reached the meadow of asphodel where dwell the souls and shadows of those who can work no more."(*Od.*, XXIV, 1–14)
32. Rohde, *Psyche*, p 7.
33. *Od.*, IV, 795 ff.
34. *Od.*, XIX, 560 ff.

35. Artemidorus, *The Interpretation of Dreams*.
36. Rohde, *Psyche*, p 7.
37. Where dreams are concerned, it would be more accurate to say the countries surrounding Hades.

The Risk of Knowledge

1. Colli, *La sapienza greca*, vol I, p 93.
2. Alcmaeon, fragment B2.
3. Quoted in: F. Càssola, *Inni Omerici*. On the secrecy of these myths, cf also Plutarch, *De defectu oraculorum*, in *Dialoghi delfici*, ed D Del Corno, Milan, Adelphi, 1983.
4. C Kerényi, 'The Mysteries of the Kabeiroi', in: Joseph Campbell, Ed: *Papers from the Eranos Yearbooks, Eranos 2. The Mysteries*, pp 38–9.
5. Colli, *La sapienza greca*, vol I, pp 92–93.
6. *Ibid*, p 28.
7. *Ibid*.
8. Cf *The Poems of St John of the Cross*,
9. Hesiod, *Works and Days*,756.
10. Euripides, *Hypsipile*, fr 57, quoted in: Colli, *La Sapienza Greca*, Vol I, p 136.
11. The veil "conveys the meaning of the separation of one thing from another and hence, depending on whether one puts on or removes the veil, it has the meaning of hidden or revealed knowledge." J Chevalier – A Gheerbrant, *Dictionnaire des symboles*, Paris, Robert Laffont-Jupiter, 1973, *s v Voile*. [*A Dictionary of Symbols*, trans John Buchanan-Brown, Oxford 1994, (original edition 1973) p 1062]
12. C Kerényi, *loc cit* See also J Burckhardt, *The Greeks and Greek Civilisation*, p 211.
13. C Kerényi, *op cit*, p 40.

14. "In fact it filters the light to make it perceptible." J Chevalier – A Gheerbrant, *Dictionnaire des symboles*, cit., *s.v. Voile*. Cf also M.Foucault, *Naissance de la clinique*, Paris, Presses universitaires de France, coll. «Quadrige», 1993, p. 170: "L'élément caché prend la forme et le rythme du contenu caché, ce qui fait qu'il est de la nature même du voile d'être transparent: le but des anatomistes 'est atteint lorsque les opaques enveloppes qui couvrent nos parties ne sont plus à leurs yeux exercés qu'un voile transparent qui laisse à découvert l'ensemble et les rapports'." And, as a note: "Dans sa silhouette générale, [cette structure] domine les formes du savoir et de l'érotisme."
15. Kerényi, 'The Mysteries of the Kabeiroi', p 39.
16. Colli, *La sapienza greca*, vol II, pp 80–81.
17. *Ibid*, pp 275–276.
18. Kerényi, *op cit*, p 40.
19. Cf Colli, *La sapienza greca*, cit, vol II, pp 22–23. Of great importance here is Schuhl's assertion in *Essai sur la formation de la pensée grecque*, Paris, Alcan, 1934, pp 148–149: "Il semble bien qu'il s'agisse ici d'un mythe démiurgique où le monde serait considéré comme un manteau divin. Peut-être est-ce par de telles représentations qu'il faut expliquer le rôle du tissage dans la mythologie des Moires, qui tissent la trame du destin, de telle sorte que tout homme doit subir." [It appears that this a demiurgic myth in which the world is considered as a divine cloak. It is probably through these representations that we must explain the role of weaving in the mythology of the Moiras, who weave the web of fate, which all men must undergo.] Cf also Detienne-Vernant, *Cunning Intelligence in Greek Culture*, p 138.
20. *Od*, V, 343 ff.
21. Cf Kerényi, *Gli dèi e gli eroi della Grecia*, Milano, Garzanti, 1976 (ed or 1963), p 243. For the loosening of the veil in the high

sea with the duty of turning back the gaze, cf the condition of mortals entering Hades alive (episode of Orpheus).

22. Nonnos, *Dionysiaca*, VI, 172–173, in: Colli, *La sapienza greca*, vol I, p 250.

23. Clement of Alexandria, *Protrepticus*, II, 17–18, in: Colli, *La sapienza greca*: "The mysteries of Dionysus are entirely inhuman; around him, while he was still a child, the Curetes danced, clashing their weapons, and the Titans crept up on them by stealth, and having deceived him with childish toys, those same Titans tore him limb from limb even though he was only a child, as the poet of the initiation, the Thracian Orpheus, says: 'The Cone, and the spinning-top, and the flexible dolls and the fair golden apples from the clear-voiced Hesperides.' And it might be worth mentioning as incriminating objects the useless symbols of this initiation: dice, ball, hoop, apples, top, looking-glass, tuft of wool."

24. Proclus, *On the Timaeus*, p 193, Vol III in: Colli, *La sapienza greca*, vol I, p 251.

25. Colli, *La sapienza greca*, p 42.

26. Chevalier - Gheerbrant, *A Dictionary of Symbols*, p 657 (s v *Mirror*).

27. J. Baltrušaitis, *Le miroir*, Paris, 1978, p 12.

28. Colli, *La sapienza greca*, cit, vol I, p 42.

29. E R Dodds, *The Greeks and the Irrational*, Berkeley, 1951, p 94

30. M Vegetti, *Il coltello e lo stilo*, Milan, il Saggiatore, 1979.

31. F Nietzsche, *Beyond Good and Evil*, trans Marion Faber, Oxford 1998, aphorism 40.

32. V Macchioro, *Zagreus. Studi intorno all'Orfismo*, Bari, Laterza, 1920, pp 94–95. Cf also Kerényi, *Miti e misteri*, pp 456–458.

33. J-P Vernant, 'Death in the Eyes', in: *Mortals and Immortals, Collected Essays*, Ed Froma I Zeitlin, Princeton 1991 (original edition 1985), p 135.

34. *Ibid*, p 137.
35. *Ibid*, p 138.

The Deception of the Spinx

1. Detienne - Vernant, *Cunning Intelligence in Greek Culture and Society*, p 18.
2. In combination with *metis* the adjective *poikilos* is in fact an essential attribute of Odysseus and Hermes.
3. J-P Vernant - P Vidal-Naquet, *Myth and Tragedy in Ancient Greece*, New York 1990, pp 207–8.
4. Cf vv 284–286: "I know that Lord Teiresias sees the future as does Lord Phoebus: investigating this matter with his help, Sire, we might know with all certainty."
5. Teiresias and Oedipus are symbols of this pessimism.
6. Cf Also Lucian, *Dialogues of the Dead,* 'Menippus and Teiresias'.
7. Plato, *Theaetetus*, 174a.
8. Kerényi, *Miti e misteri*, p 215.
9. M Heidegger, *The Saying of Anaximander*, in *idem*, *Off the Beaten Track*, Ed and trans Julian Young and Kenneth Haynes, Cambridge 2002 (orig ed 1950), p 250: "In order to translate ourselves into that which comes into language in the saying we must, prior to all translating, consciously set aside all inappropriate preconceptions. For example, that the saying deals with the philosophy of nature in such a way that inappropriate notions from morality and the law are mixed into the discussion. Or, finally, that a primitive outlook still prevails in the saying which interprets the world uncritically and anthropomorphically, and therefore takes refuge in poetic expressions.)"
10. Cf Heidegger, *The Saying of Anaximander*, ibid, p 259: "The experience of beings in their being which here comes to language is

neither pessimistic nor nihilistic. Nor is it optimistic. It remains tragic."
11. R M Rilke, Eighth Duino Elegy.
12. Cf Dodds, *The Greeks and the Irrational*, pp 64–101.
13. *Od.*, VIII, 63 ff.
14. I will address this transformation in Chapter 7. Cf also Heidegger, '*Plato's Doctrine of Truth*'.
15. R M Rilke, untitled poem, quoted in, M Heidegger, op cit, p 109.

The Invisible Connection

1. *Logos dynastis megas estin, os smikrotatoi somati kai aphanestatoi theiotata erga apotelei.*
2. Cf G Colli, *La nascita della filosofia*, Milano, Adelphi, 1975.
3. *Loxias* means the Oblique one, if we interpret it according to the epithet *loxos*. C Ramnoux, *La nuit et les enfants de la Nuit dans la tradition grecque*, Paris, Flammarion, 1959, p 182.
4. Colli, *La nascita della filosofia*, cit, p 18.
5. Cf Plato, *Symposium*, 216a: the play of wisdom and deception is contained within the comparison between the song of the Sirens and that of Socrates.
6. Colli, *La Sapienza greca*, p 18.
7. Cf E Zeller - R Mondolfo, *La filosofia dei greci nel suo sviluppo storico*, Firenze, La Nuova Italia, 1961, vol IV, Part 1, p 90: "When B45 says that the limits of the soul are unreachable, he may not be thinking of the problem of self-knowledge so much as the soul as a portion of cosmic fire." Cf also M Heidegger – E Fink, *Heraclitus Seminar*, trans Charles H Seibert, Evanston Illinois 1993, p 90: "I am of the opinion that the soul in the sense of the human soul is not primarily what is meant by *psychai*. An element of endowment with consciousness does not enter into the activity of the elements with *psychai*."

8. Cf Rilke, '*Eighth Duino Elegy*', cf also C Sini, *Passare il segno*, Milano, il Saggiatore, 1981, p 71.
9. The term 'language' is too loaded, today, with meanings alien to ancient Greek thought..
10. Cf Heidegger - Fink, *The Heraclitus Seminar*, p 120.
11. A negative reading of the passage is also possible.

The Gift Of Mnemosyne

1. Colli, *La sapienza greca*, vol II, p 52.
2. *Ibid*, vol II, p 49.
3. *Ibid*, p 67.
4. Diogenes Laertius, *Lives of Eminent Philosophers*, trans in: G Colli, *La sapienza greca*, vol II, p 55.
5. Jean-Pierre Vernant, *Myth and Thought among the Greeks*, London 1983 (original edition 1973), p 76.
6. One early historical examination of the theme of time occurs in Aristotle. It is only with him that the 'biological criterion' comes to be applied, according to which "human thought, and philosophical thought in particular, passes from less perfect to more perfect forms; which amounts to saying that it has a natural life of its own, a continuity of its own, regulated by a fundamental necessity beyond the contingent." But we may still assert that "Aristotle is the first thinker who is aware of his own historicity". (F Decleva Caizzi, *Cenni sul tema della verità e della storia in Aristotele*, in *Materiali per una riflessione sul problema della storia presso i Greci*, ed G Turrini, 1975–1976, Dispensa del corso di Storia della filosofia antica, pp 81–85).
7. C G Jung and K Kerényi, *Introduction to a Science of Mythology: The Divine Child and the Mysteries of Eleusis*, London 1951, pp 9–32.
8. J-P Vernant, *Myth and Thought Among the Greeks*, p 80.

9. Jung - Kerényi, *Introduction to a Science of Mythology*, pp 9–32.
10. To reach the idea of 'progress', one must have a historical conception of time and that, as we have seen above, begins with Aristotle.
11. If connected to the root *ìd-*, *Aìdes* means 'invisible'.
12. The potency of this helmet has the fearsomeness of the face of the Gorgon.
13. Kerényi, *Gli dèi e gli eroi della Grecia*, p 296.
14. *Phàos àskopon* in Euripides, *Hypsipile*, 157ff.
15. "Well-meaning modern efforts to read a moral meaning into things Greek have sought to prove that the Greeks, too, had a genuine popular believe in a future judgment and recompense for the past deeds and character of the dead." And again: "Nor were [the Greeks] very susceptible during their best centuries to the infectious malady of a "sick conscience". What had they do with pictures of an underworld of purgatory and torment in expiation of all imaginary types and degrees of sin, as in Dante's ghastly Hell? It is true that even such dark fancies of the Christian Hell are in part derived from Greek sources. But it was only the misguided fancy of particular isolated sects that could call forth such pictures as these, and recommend itself to a philosophic speculation which in its worst excesses violently contradicted all the most fundamental principles of Greek culture. The people and the religion of Greece, the mysteries which her cities organised and deemed holy, may be freely acquitted of all such aberrations." (Rohde, *Psyche*, pp 238 and 242).
16. Rohde, *Psyche*, p 239..
17. Kerényi, *The Heroes of the Greeks*, p 284.
18. Colli, *La sapienza greca*, vol I. The gold leaf dates back to 400 BC, and was found at Ipponio in Southern Italy.

19. Cf Colli, *La sapienza greca*, vol I, pp 39–40.
20. This is the meaning of the episode of Odysseus and the Sirens. He has chosen life over knowledge, in that the song he listens to while tied to the mast of the ship does not constitute knowledge, but instead means the impossibility on his part of acquiring it.
21. The underlying sentiment is nostalgia. Cf A Chekhov, *Collected Works*, and above, *Postface*.
22. Rilke, *Eighth Duino Elegy*.

The Charlatans of Heaven

1. Anassagora, Fr. A18
2. Plato, *Laws,* 967c.
3. *Ibid.*
4. [way of going from the visible to the invisible] P M Schuhl, *Adèla*, p 89.
5. M Heidegger, 'Science and Reflection', in: *The Question Concerning Technology and Other Essays*, trans William Lovitt, New York, 1997, p 164. "For the Greeks, the point of view of the spectator is in itself divine: for them, to assume it simply means the divine completeness of existence; the philosophers look upon it and hope to reach that completeness. The reason for their hope, however, is enclosed within the character of the Greek religious experience: for the Greeks, festivity and spectator's point of view are indissolubly united. They use the solemn word 'spectator', *teoròs*: person who sees a vision (*teà*), even the participant in the festival. The attainability of this divine point of view is not guaranteed by mystical experiences, but by this fundamental experience of festive religiosity: that is, by the experience that festivity raises to divinity. If their philosophers temporarily occupy that point of view – not like the gods in a festival lasting

for ever – they attain it in the quality of festive men, men of *teorìa*."

6. "Suppressing distance kills. The gods only die in our midst." R Char, *L'Age cassant*, Paris, Jose Corti, 1966.

7. Schuhl, *Essai sur la formation de la pensée grecque*, p 329, says: "Le *Nous* est avant tout – le nom même l'indique – pensée, connaissance pure: on ne saurait s'étonner que celui qui passa pour faire de la contemplation du monde la fin de la vie humaine ait établi au centre de la réalité l'intelligence discriminatrice; ces éléments minuscules qui échappent à nos sens et que notre pensée devine à peine, le *Nous* les connaît: la toute puissance que lui prête Anaxagore signifiescience, d'après Aristote. Néanmoins il n'est pas immatériel – pas plus que le Logos enflammé d'Héraclite: comme les qualités, il est une chose – la plus pure et la plus subtile de toutes – mais une chose: spiritualisme et matérialisme ne sont pas encore 'séparés'" [*Nous* is primarily – as the very name suggests – thought, pure knowledge: we should not be surprised that anyone who claimed to make the contemplation of the world the goal of human life should have placed discriminating intelligence at the centre of reality; those tiny elements that escape our senses, and of which our thought is barely aware, are known to *Nous*: the omnipotence granted to it by Anaxagoras signifies science, according to Aristotle. Nonetheless it is not immaterial – any more than the inflamed *Logos* of Heraclitus: like the qualities, it is a thing – the purest and must subtle of all – but still just a thing: spiritualism and materialism are not yet separated.]

8. Vegetti, *Il coltello e lo stilo*, pp 27–28.

9. In this respect it has the same power as Athena.

10. Cf Sophocles, *Oedipus the King*.

11. Plato, *Phaedrus*, 244a.

12. A35.

13. Cf A Montano, *Il fenomeno e il discorso: il modello epistemologico di Democrito*, in: *Democrito. Dall'atomo alla città*, Ed G Casertano, Naples, 2002, p 80.
14. P M Schuhl, *Adèla*.
15. G Giorello, *Lo spettro e il libertino*, Milan, 1985, p 301.

The Paradox of Perception

1. Cf M. Detienne, *The Creation of Mythology*, trans Margaret Cook, Chicago 1986 (original edition 1981), pp 93–105.
2. It is curious to note how this characteristic runs parallel, but in a diametrically opposite sense, to Penelope's cloth.
3. Herodotus, *Histories*, IV, 36.
4. When we use the name Hippocrates we are referring to what is generally understood as the *Corpus Hippocraticum*. More than any chronological or biographical controversies, I am concerned here to get to the heart of some points of Hippocratic doctrine, aware of the limits that it may involve with regard to a more precise discourse.
5. M Foucault, *Birth of the Clinic*, p 107.
6. 'It is in medicine, moreover, that we find the beginnings of a genuinely experimental procedure' (F. M Cornford, *Principium Sapientiae: the Origin of Greek Philosophical Thought*, New York, Cambridge University Press, 1952, p 38).
7. "The semantic method was configured thus, for the Hippocratic *tékne* as a 'dialectical' movement which, proceeding from the *ékaston* posited by observation (although nowadays it would be more appropriate to speak of scientific 'experiment') transformed it into *semeìon* via a logical and conceptual inference (*logismòs*), and then into proof or *tekmérion*, to conclude, if the circle was had been completed, in the capacity for practical intervention on ever new *ékasta*." (M Vegetti, in Ippocrate, *Opere*, pp 40–41)
8. M Foucault, Birth of the Clinic, p. 110.

9. *Ibid*, p 109.
10. *Ibid*, p 204.
11. Alcmaeon, A10.
12. It is a reproach similar to the one that the slave-girl makes to Thales when he falls into the well. But its significance is diametrically opposite.

The Double Vision

1. Chantraine, *Dictionnaire étymologique de la langue grecque: histoire des mots*, s v *eidos*.
2. As far as we can ascertain from dictionaries. In Platonic *theoria* the three words of the classical sages are concentrated in a single one.
3. Plato, *Phaedo*, 83b.
4. Rilke, *Eighth Duino Elegy*.
5. Cf Plato, *Phaedo*, 67c-70d.
6. Cf Sini, *Passare il segno*, pp 293–295.
7. Plato, *Theaetetus*, 1521 ff.
8. Plato, *Phaedrus*, 230a.
9. G W Hegel, *Phenomenology of Spirit*, trans A V Miller, Oxford, Clarendon Press, p 124.

Heracles at the Crossroads

1. Nietzsche, *The Birth of Tragedy*, p 115.
2. The Gospel of Philip, trans Wesley W Isenberg, v 52, in: *The Nag Hammadi Library in English*, Leiden 1996, p 140.
3. Nietzsche, *The Birth of Tragedy*, p 46.
4. I am referring to the admirable work by Colli, *La sapienza greca*.
5. Pascal, *Pensées*, trans J M Cohen, Harmondsworth 1961, 84, pp 51–2.
6. Plato, *The Republic*, 514a.
7. Cf J Van Eyck, *The Arnolfini Wedding*, 1434.

8. ['There is no science but of the hidden'] L Gernet, *Choses visibles et choses invisibles*, in Revue Philosophique", 1956, p 80.
9. Giorello, *Lo spettro e il libertino*, p 301.
10. 'The Scientific Conception of the World. The Vienna Circle' in: Sarkar, Sahotra (Ed) *The Emergence of Logical Empiricism from 1900 to the Vienna Circle*, New York, 1996, pp 321–40.
11. H von Hofmannsthal, *Aufzeichnungen*, Frankfurt 1957, p 47.
12. Goethe, *Faust*, Part I, trans David Luke, Oxford, 1987, pp 41–2.

Postface
1. Cf Ch. 1.
2. Cf T W Adorno, *Minima Moralia. Meditations from Damaged Life*, trans E F N Jephcott, London 1974. Adorno writes (78, p 121) "Truth is inseparable from the illusory belief that from the figures of the unreal one day, in spite of all, real deliverance will come."
3. Cf Ch 5.

BIBLIOGRAPHY

AESCHYLUS, *Oresteia*

ANASSAGORA, *Testimonianze e frammenti*

ARISTOTLE, *Metafisica*

ARTEMIDORUS, *The Interpretation of Dreams*

G. COLLI, *La sapienza greca, Milano, Adelphi, 1977–1980*

HERODOTUS, *The Histories*

HESIOD, *Theogony and Works and Days*

HIPPOCRATES, *Antica medicina, in Id., Opere*

HOMER, *The Iliad*

HOMER, *The Odyssey*

I PRESOCRATICI, *Testimonianze e frammenti*

LUCIAN, *Selected Dialogues*

OVID, *Metamorphoses*

PLATO, *Cratylus*

PLATO, *Phaedo*

PLATO, *Phaedrus*

PLATO, *The Republic*

SOPHOCLES, *Oedipus the King*

ILLUSTRATIONS

p. 17 – The armour of Achilles

p. 29 – The deception of Hephaestus

p. 41 – Heracles veiled

p. 49 – The myth of Narcissus

p. 55 – The Silenus and the mask

p. 69 – The riddle of the Sphinx

p. 79 – The song of the Sirens

p. 87 – The face of the Gorgon

p. 103 – The ghost of Athena

p. 111 – The appearance of Thetis

p. 123 – The eclipse of the sun

p. 135 – The women of Heracles

I owe a massive debt of gratitude to Giuseppe Pontiggia, without whom this book would not have been conceived. His subsequent support has also been crucial. The same holds for Guido Turrini, with his brilliant philological intuitions, and Carlo Sini, who, reading the final draft years later, confirmed his opinion and reinforced mine. I then thank my father for my first important discussions on the relationship between appearance and being, Umberto Pasti, a severe and attentive reader, whose advice on the structure of the sentences and the choice of some words has been inescapable, Angelo Manfredi, the 'upbeat' poet, Vittorio Lingiardi for the definition (his or mine) of the 'myth-rodent', Carlo Pecora, my almost daily lunch companion, RM and LS because they have been and remain the landscape of my life.

Pushkin Press

Pushkin Press was founded in 1997. Having first rediscovered European classics of the twentieth century, Pushkin now publishes novels, essays, memoirs, children's books, and everything from timeless classics to the urgent and contemporary.

Pushkin Paper books, like this one, represent exciting, high-quality writing from around the world. Pushkin publishes widely acclaimed, brilliant authors such as Stefan Zweig, Marcel Aymé, Antal Szerb, Paul Morand and Hermann Hesse, as well as some of the most exciting contemporary and often prize-winning writers, including Andrés Neuman, Ellen Ullman, Eduardo Halfon and Ryu Murakami.

Pushkin Press publishes the world's best stories, to be read and read again.

*

HÉCTOR ABAD	*Recipes for Sad Women*
OLIVIER ADAM	*Cliffs*
FLAVIA ARZENI	*An Education in Happiness:*
	The Lessons of Hesse and Tagore
FRANÇOIS AUGIÉRAS	*A Journey to Mount Athos*
	Journey of the Dead
	The Sorcerer's Apprentice
MARCEL AYMÉ	*Beautiful Image*
	The Man Who Walked through Walls
SALIM BACHI	*The New Adventures of Sinbad the Sailor*
	The Silence of Mohammed
PHILIPPE BEAUSSANT	*Rendezvous in Venice*
ANDREI BELY	*Petersburg*
OLIVIER BERGGRUEN	*The Writing of Art*
EDUARDO BERTI	*Agua*

FILIPPO BOLOGNA	*How I Lost the War*
	The Parrots
MARELLA CARACCIOLO CHIA	*The Light in Between*
VELIBOR ČOLIĆ	*The Uncannily Strange and Brief Life of Amedeo Modigliani*
LOUIS COUPERUS	*Ecstasy*
	Eline Vere
	Inevitable
	Psyche
	The Hidden Force
RÉGIS DEBRAY	*Against Venice*
PENELOPE S. DELTA	*A Tale Without a Name*
CHARLES DICKENS	*Memoirs of Joseph Grimaldi*
ISAK DINESEN	*The Necklace and The Pearls*
ALAIN ELKANN	*Envy*
	The French Father
NICOLAS FARGUES	*I Was behind You*
MEDARDO FRAILE	*Things Look Different in the Light and Other Stories*
CARLOS GAMERRO	*An Open Secret*
JULIEN GRACQ	*A Dark Stranger*
	Chateau d'Argol
JULIAN GREEN	*The Other Sleep*
BROTHERS GRIMM	*The Juniper Tree and Other Tales*
PIETRO GROSSI	*Fists*
	The Break
	Enchantment
EDUARDO HALFON	*The Polish Boxer*
PETER HANDKE	*A Sorrow Beyond Dreams*
HERMANN HESSE	*Hymn to Old Age*
E.T.A. HOFFMANN	*The Nutcracker and The Strange Child*
HUGO VON HOFMANNSTHAL	*Andreas*
HENRY JAMES	*Letters from the Palazzo Barbaro*
	Letters to Isabella Stewart Gardner
PETER STEPHAN JUNGK	*The Inheritance*
ERLING KAGGE	*Philosophy for Polar Explorers*
SØREN KIERKEGAARD	*Diary of a Seducer*
PETR KRÁL	*In Search of the Essence of Place*
	Loving Venice
	Working Knowledge
SIMON LIBERATI	*Anthology of Apparitions*

Oliver Matuschek	*Three Lives: A Biography of Stefan Zweig*
Guy de Maupassant	*The Necklace and The Pearls*
Jean-Euphèle Milcé	*Alphabet of the Night*
Paul Morand	*Hecate and Her Dogs*
	Tender Shoots
	The Allure of Chanel
	Venices
Ryu Murakami	*Popular Hits from the Showa Era*
	From the Fatherland with Love
	Coin Locker Babies
	69
Andrés Neuman	*Traveller of the Century*
Umberto Pasti	*The Age of Flowers*
Edith Pearlman	*Binocular Vision*
Edgar Allan Poe	*The Journal of Julius Rodman*
Alexander Pushkin	*The Queen of Spades and Selected Works*
Raymond Radiguet	*Count d'Orgel*
	The Devil in the Flesh
Antoine de Saint-Exupéry	*Letter to a Hostage*
George Sand	*Laura: A Journey into the Crystal*
Friedrich von Schiller	*The Man Who Sees Ghosts*
Arthur Schnitzler	*Casanova's Return to Venice*
	Dying
	Fräulein Else
Adolf Schröder	*The Game of Cards*
William Shakespeare	*Sonnets*
Nihad Sirees	*The Silence and the Roar*
Jan Jacob Slauerhoff	*The Forbidden Kingdom*
Simona Sparaco	*About Time*
Adalbert Stifter	*The Bachelors*
	Rock Crystal
Italo Svevo	*A Life*
Antal Szerb	*Journey by Moonlight*
	Love in a Bottle
	Oliver VII
	The Pendragon Legend
	The Queen's Necklace
Friedrich Torberg	*Young Gerber*
Mark Twain	*The Jumping Frog and Other Sketches*

ELLEN ULLMAN	*By Blood*
	Close to the Machine
	The Bug
LOUISE DE VILMORIN	*Madame de*
ERNST WEISS	*Franziska*
	Jarmila
EDITH WHARTON	*Glimpses of the Moon*
FLORIAN ZELLER	*Artificial Snow*
	Julien Parme
	Lovers or Something Like It
	The Fascination of Evil
STEFAN ZWEIG	*Amok and Other Stories*
	Beware of Pity
	Burning Secret
	Casanova: A Study in Self-Portraiture
	Confusion
	Fear
	Journey into the Past
	Letter from an Unknown Woman and Other Stories
	Magellan
	Marie Antoinette
	Mary Stuart
	Mental Healers: Mesmer, Eddy, Freud
	Selected Stories
	The Governess and Other Stories
	The Royal Game
	The Struggle with the Daemon: Hölderlin, Kleist, Nietzsche
	The World of Yesterday
	Twilight and Moonbeam Alley
	Wondrak and Other Stories